CAMBRIDGE
Global English

Learner's Book

2

Caroline Linse and Elly Schottman

CAMBRIDGE
UNIVERSITY PRESS

CAMBRIDGE
UNIVERSITY PRESS

University Printing House, Cambridge CB2 8BS, United Kingdom

One Liberty Plaza, 20th Floor, New York, NY 10006, USA

477 Williamstown Road, Port Melbourne, VIC 3207, Australia

314–321, 3rd Floor, Plot 3, Splendor Forum, Jasola District Centre, New Delhi – 110025, India

79 Anson Road, #06–04/06, Singapore 079906

Cambridge University Press is part of the University of Cambridge.

It furthers the University's mission by disseminating knowledge in the pursuit of education, learning and research at the highest international levels of excellence.

www.cambridge.org
Information on this title: www.cambridge.org/9781107613805

© Cambridge University Press 2016

First published 2014

20 19 18 17

Printed in Dubai by Oriental Press

A catalogue record for this publication is available from the British Library

ISBN 978-1-107-61380-5 Learner's Book with Audio CDs (2)

Additional resources for this publication at www.cambridge.org

Cambridge University Press has no responsibility for the persistence or accuracy of URLs for external or third-party internet websites referred to in this publication, and does not guarantee that any content on such websites is, or will remain, accurate or appropriate. Information regarding prices, travel timetables, and other factual information given in this work is correct at the time of first printing but Cambridge University Press does not guarantee the accuracy of such information thereafter.

Welcome to Cambridge Global English Stage 2

Cambridge Global English is an eight-stage course for learners of English as a Second Language (ESL). The eight stages range from the beginning of primary (Stages 1–6) to the end of the first two years of junior secondary (Stages 7–8). It is ideal for all international ESL learners, and particularly for those following the Cambridge Primary/Secondary English as a Second Language Curriculum Framework, as it has been written to adhere to this framework. It also presents realistic listening and reading texts, writing tasks and end-of-unit projects similar to those students might encounter in the context of a first-language school. These elements provide teachers with the opportunity to tailor the level of challenge to meet the needs of their particular students. The course is organised into nine thematic units of study which include a range of activities, text types and objectives.

Cambridge Global English materials are aligned with the Common European Framework of Reference. The materials reflect the following principles:

- *An international focus*. Specifically developed for young learners throughout the world, the topics and situations in *Cambridge Global English* have been selected to reflect this diversity and encourage learning about each other's lives through the medium of English.
- *An enquiry-based, language-rich approach to learning*. *Cambridge Global English* engages children as active, creative learners. At the same time as participating in a range of curriculum-based activities, they can acquire content knowledge, develop critical thinking skills, and practise English language and literacy.

- *English for educational success*. To meet the challenges of the future, learners will need to develop facility with both conversational and more formal English. From the earliest stage, *Cambridge Global English* addresses both these competencies. Emphasis is placed on developing the listening, speaking, reading and writing skills learners will need to be successful in using English-language classroom materials.

In addition to this Learner's Book, *Cambridge Global English Activity Book 2* provides supplementary support and practice. Comprehensive support for teachers is available in *Cambridge Global English Teacher's Resource 2*.

The following icons are used in this Learner's Book:

- **1** pre-recorded listening activity
- pre-recorded song and class singing activity
- pairwork or small group speaking activity (not mediated by teacher)
- write in notebook activity
- **AB** linking activity in Activity Book
- **1+2** cross-curricular maths activity
- cross-curricular science activity.

We hope that learners and teachers enjoy using *Cambridge Global English Stage 2* as much as we have enjoyed writing it.

Caroline Linse and Elly Schottman

Contents

page	Unit	Words and expressions	Use of English	Reading/Writing
6–19	1 Look in a book	Books and parts of a book Classroom objects Numbers 1–15 Clothes and personal possessions *What is it about?* *How do you spell …?* *How do you say __ in English?*	Singular/plural nouns *There is/are …* Present simple Possessive pronouns (*mine, yours*) Genitive *'s* *have got* + noun *like* + *-ing* *Which one?* / *the __ one*	Poems/songs Information text Write personal information Write about your school Write an original song verse Use a capital letter and full stop
20–33	2 Good neighbours	People and places in the community Extended family Places in the world Jobs Shops Ordinal numbers *Left, right* *A lot of*	Present continuous Question forms Present simple 3rd person endings: *-s, -es* Irregular plurals Prepositions of location	Poems/songs Information text Write a friendly letter Report information from an interview Write instructions collaboratively
34–47	3 Ready, steady, go!	Action verbs Parts of the body Numbers 1–20 Feelings (adjectives)	Imperatives *Can/can't* for ability Adverbs: *slowly, quickly* Conjunctions: *and, but, or* Determiners: *all, most, some* *I like /don't like* + verb + *-ing*	Poems/songs Information text Play: Native American tale Write information about birds Write an original song verse Write a riddle
48–61	4 The big sky	Weather Shadows Day and night: *Sun, Moon, stars, planets* Time phrases: *Yesterday, in the morning, at night* Movement verbs	Past simple regular (*-ed*) and irregular forms Past simple of *be* Past simple question forms Time expressions: *in the morning/ afternoon/evening; at night*	Poems/songs Information text Read and follow instructions Write informational sentences Report interview information (past tense)
62–75	5 Let's count and measure	Numbers 1–100 *How many? How far? How long?* *Metres, centimetres* Shapes Tell time to the hour	Past simple regular and irregular forms Countable and uncountable nouns with *some, a/an* *What (a)* + adj. + noun*!* *When* clause	Poems and song Information text Traditional stories from India and Africa Write personal information Write a new verse
76–89	6 Bugs: fact and fiction	Insects and spiders Parts of insects (wings, legs, antennae) Action verbs	Prepositions: *above, under, near, on* Determiners: *all, some, most* Subject/verb agreement Regular and irregular past tense *How, What, How many, Do/Does?*	Poems/songs Information text Traditional story from Mexico Story elements: Plot (story map) Describe insects and what they do Write questions
90–103	7 Our green Earth	Parks, leisure time Parts of a tree Fruits and vegetables Environmental issues *Would you like …? I'd/We'd like …* *How about …?* *What does __ mean?*	*-ing* forms as nouns (*no + -ing* form) *Must/mustn't* with rules/instructions *Can* for permission *Will* for future intentions/promises Determiners: *this, these, that, those*	Poems/songs Information text Write promises/intentions Write a poem Write your autobiography
104–117	8 Home, sweet home	Parts of a building Kinds of homes Climates (hot, cold, warm, cool, wet, dry) Rooms and furnishings Animal homes Construction materials *What is it made of?*	Present perfect *have* + object + infinitive *Have you ever…?* *Let's* and *How about* + *-ing* for suggestions *Would you like __ or __ ? I'd like…* *Too* to add information *Will* for future intention	Poems Narrative song Information text Information from diagrams Write descriptions of things Narrative writing (retell story)
118–131	9 Inside and outside cities	Buildings and other city words Holiday places and leisure activities Food and drink Opposites	*Where/what would you like to …?* Comparative adjectives: *-er* and *more* + adjective; *better* Expressing agreement/disagreement: *So do I! I don't*	Poems/songs Information text Fable from Aesop (contemporary retelling) Write a poem (*haiku*) Write a picture caption (stating and explaining a preference)
132–143	Picture dictionary	Review of vocabulary and themes		

Listening/Speaking	School subjects	Phonics / Word study	Critical thinking / Values

Listen for information
Follow instructions
Ask and answer questions
Collaborative problem solving
Memory games
Ask about an unknown word
	Maths: Counting
	Using a contents page
	Using a dictionary
		Letter names and sounds
		Vowels and consonants
		Sounds: *sh, ch, th*
		Short vowel sounds in initial
		  and middle position
		Spelling dictation
		Compound words
			What can you find in a book?
			Classifying
			Main ideas and details
			Values: Taking care of books and school
			  supplies (responsibility, respect)

Listen for information
Ask for, give and follow directions
Roleplay + guessing game
Interviews
	Social studies: Communities
	Geography: Reading maps,
	  using a map grid
		Occupation words ending
		  with *-er. singer, writer,* etc.
		Prefix *un-*
			Who lives in your neighbourhood?
			Asking interview questions
			Interpreting maps
			Values: In a caring community, people
			  help each other

Listen to and give instructions
Discuss likes and dislikes
Discuss and act out poems, song
  and play
	Science: Different bird
	  species; interpreting
	  a chart
	Maths: Counting
	Physical education: Moving
	  different parts of the body
		Long vowel sounds and
		  spellings: *ai, ay;* silent *e*
			How can we move in different ways?
			Comparing and contrasting
			Classifying
			Values: Teamwork; an active life style
			  keeps us healthy and happy

Listen for information
Ask/answer questions
Partner interviews
Discuss and act out poems and song
	Science: Shadows; weather;
	  day and night; Earth,
	  Moon, Sun and planets
		Long *i* spellings: *i, igh*
		Rhyming words
		Spelling dictation
		Compound words
			What is the sky like?
			Making and using a sundial
			Comparing and contrasting
			Values: Appreciating and learning about
			  the natural world

Listen for information
Ask/answer questions
Memory games
Discuss and act out poems, songs
  and stories
	Maths: Counting in 2s;
	  measuring, completing
	  chart, telling the time
	  (to the hour); shapes
		Homophones	*How do we use numbers?*
			Problem solving
			Sequencing
			Estimating
			Values: We can work together to help
			  ourselves learn

Listen for information
Ask/answer questions
Discuss and act out poems, songs and
  stories
Insect game
	Science: Insects and spiders	Long *e* spellings (*ee, ea,
		  me, s/he*)
		Rhyming words
			How are bugs special?
			Classifying
			Comparing
			Study skills
			Graphic organisers
			Values: Appreciating and learning about
			  the natural world

Listen for information
Give/follow instructions
Ask/answer questions
Discuss and apply information
Discuss and act out poems and song
	Science and Social studies:
	  Environmental issues; uses
	  of trees
	Social studies: International
	  signs
	Science: Plants; growing food
		Long *o* spellings
		  (*ou* and *ow*)
		Variant sounds of *ow*
			How can we care for the Earth?
			Problem solving
			Sequencing
			Study skills
			Values: We are responsible for taking
			  care of the Earth

Listen for information
Ask/answer questions
Share information
Make decisions and choices
Recite and discuss poems and song
	Social studies: Homes around
	  the world
	Geography: World places and
	  climates
	Science: Homes built by
	  animals; building materials
		Long *u* spellings: Variant
		  sounds of *oo*
		Rhyming words
			*What kinds of homes do people and
			  animals build?*
			Collaborative learning
			Values: Homes offer shelter and safety
			Homes around the world are both similar
			  and unique

Listen for information
Recognise speaker's opinion
Problem solving
Discuss preferences
Roleplay: Ask for food and drink
Discuss and act out poem, song
  and story
	Geography: Mountains,
	  beach, desert, etc.
	Social studies: Community
	  places in a city
		Identify opposites
		Count syllables
		Variant sounds of *c*
			*What can we do in the town and
			  countryside?*
			Comparing
			Supporting an opinion with reasons
			Values: Respecting different opinions
			  and preferences

1 Look in a book

1 Think about it   What can you find in a book?

2 1 Read and listen

Which story has stayed inside your head?

3 2 💬 Which book?

Look at the books in the picture.
Which one would you like to read? Why?
Then listen and point to the correct book.

Reading

A story is a special thing.
The ones that I have read,
They do not stay inside the books.
They stay inside my head.

Marchette Chute

Unit 1 Lesson 1 Vocabulary: colours and numbers review; books **Use of English:** singular and plural nouns; *There is/are*; genitive *'s* **Read/Listen:** *Reading*; aural comprehension **Talk:** questions **Write:** a book about you

3 Topic vocabulary

Listen, point and say.

Then listen and follow the instructions.

bookcase

book cover

tablet with e-book

cupboard

pages

4 💬 Colours and numbers

Ask questions about the picture on page 6.

Language tip

How many book**s** are there?

There **is one** book.

There **are two** books.

How many chairs are there?

What colour is the ruler?

5 📝 Make a book about you!

Make a cover for your book. Write your name on it, like this:

Feng's book   Sara's book

On each page, draw a picture and write about you.

2 Find out more Inside a book

Busy Boats
Jack Adler

1 A book cover

Look at the book cover.

Who is the author? What is the title?

What is the book about?

Find another book in your classroom.

Answer the questions again.

2 💬 Inside a book

Look at the contents page.

It is at the beginning of a book.

It tells you what is in the book.

This book has four chapters.

Here are four pictures from the
book *Busy Boats*. In which chapter
can you find each picture? Which page will you look at?

Contents	page
1 Little boats	2
2 Big boats	5
3 Old boats	8
4 New boats	10

a

b

c

d

Unit 1 Lesson 2 Vocabulary: fiction/non-fiction **Use of English:** prepositions; present tense; imperative; possessive adjectives; *your, our* **Read:** for information
Write: a class book about school

3 Fiction or non-fiction?

Books can be **fiction** or **non-fiction**.
Some books are fiction.
Fiction books tell a story.
The stories are not real.
Fiction books have **characters**.
Characters are the people or animals in a story.
Look at the book *The Snowy Day*. Who are the characters?

Some books are **non-fiction**. They give real information.

Look at the books on this page.

Are they fiction or non-fiction?

4 Choose a book

Choose a book for the two children.

My name is Rasha.
I like learning new things.
I like non-fiction.
My father is a pilot.

My name is Miguel.
I like reading funny
stories about animals.
I don't like scary stories.

5 A book about your school

Write a book with your class. The title is *Welcome to our school*.
The chapters could be:

Our school   Our class   Our teacher   Our classroom

3 Words and sounds Review of short vowels

5 1 ♪ Vowels and consonants

Can you remember the alphabet? Listen and sing the song.

A B C D E F G H I J K L M
N O P Q R S T U V W X Y Z

Some letters are called **vowels** and some are
called **consonants**. Can you name the vowels?
Listen and find out.

Sing the ABC song again.
This time, clap when you sing each vowel.

6 2 Vowels at the beginning

Make six cards. Write a different vowel on
each card. Say the short vowel sounds.
Listen and look at the pictures. Which vowel
do you hear at the beginning of each word?
Hold up the correct card.

7 3 Vowels in the middle

Listen and repeat these words. Which vowel sound do you
hear in the middle? Hold up the correct card.

Say a sentence for each picture.

4 💬 How do you spell it?

Choose a picture, but don't tell your partner.
Your partner must ask you the spelling.
Your partner writes down the word, says
the word and points to the picture.

> How do you spell it?
>
> p - e - n

cat	duck	cut	pan	chips
ship	shop	pen	bag	catch

8 5 [1+2] Numbers 1 to 15

Listen and count from 1 to 10.
Then listen and point to the numbers from 11 to 15.

**11 eleven   12 twelve   13 thirteen
14 fourteen   15 fifteen**

How many people are there in each picture?
Count aloud with a partner.

A

B

Talking about possessions

9 **1** 💬 **Whose backpack?**

Look at the picture. These children are on a camping holiday and their backpacks are all mixed up!
Listen. Which backpack belongs to which child?

Practise the conversation with children in your class using **yours** and **mine**.

Language tip

Is it your backpack?
= Is it **yours**?

Yes, it's my backpack.
= Yes, it's **mine**.

Which backpack?
= Which **one**?

The red backpack.
= The red **one**.

Language detective

Backpack has the word **back** in it.
You carry it on your back. It is a compound word – a big word made of two little words.
Complete the sentences below.

A **lunchbox** is a **box** with **lunch** inside.

A **classroom** is a **room** with a ___ inside.

A **bedroom** is a **room** with a ___ inside.

A **bookshop** is a **shop** that sells ___ .

2 What's in the backpack?

This is Jill's backpack.
What has she got in it?

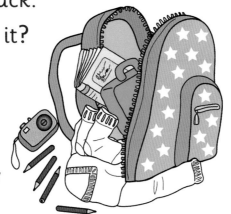

She's got a pink hairbrush.

This is Nick's backpack.
What has he got in it?

He's got two white socks.

Look at the words below
to check your answers.

hairbrush   skipping rope   camera   jumper   pencil

lunchbox   shoe   jacket   book   sock

3 Can you remember?

Choose one of the backpacks in Activity 2. Is it Jill's or Nick's?
Look in the picture at the things inside. Then close your eyes.
Tell your partner what is in the backpack.
Win a point for each thing you remember!
How many points have you got?

5 Read and respond

1 🎵 **Before you read**

Look at the picture below. Look at the title of the song.

Why do you think a book is like a window?

Is the book in the picture a fiction or a non-fiction book?

What characters are there?

Would you like to read the book?

Listen, read and sing.

This book is my window

From inside my little room

Where I dream and wonder why,

Books can open up my eyes

Like a window to the sky.

From inside my little room

Where I dream and wonder why.

As the pages turn and turn
There's so much for me to learn.
Stories, poems, recipes,
Dinosaurs and history.
As the pages turn and turn
There's so much for me to learn.

When I open up a book
Each page whispers, 'Look! Look! Look!'
Sports and monkeys, trains and kings,
Stories of amazing things.
When I open up a book
Each page whispers, 'Look! Look! Look!'

From inside my little room,
Who can tell where I will go!
Places I would like to see,
Friends that I would like to know.
When I stop and read a book,
Who can tell where I will go!

Kathryn Harper

2 How do you say it in English?

You need five small pieces of paper. Draw something that you like reading about on each. Do you know how to say those things in English?

If you don't know the word in English, you can use a dictionary or a computer or a mobile phone .

Or you can ask your teacher!

Write the English word on the back of each picture.

Then teach your words to a partner!

3 Write your own verse!

What do you like reading about? Use the words that you and your partner looked up in Activity 2 to finish these sentences. Then sing your new verse.

When I open up a book
Each page whispers, 'Look! Look! Look!'
___ and ___ , ___ and ___ ,
Stories of ___ .
When I open up a book
Each page whispers, 'Look! Look! Look!'

Words to remember

Find these words in the story:

open read when.

Practise spelling them.

6 Choose a project — What can you find in a book?

A Make a poster: Things we like reading about

- Think of a lot of things you like reading about. Write words and draw pictures on the poster.

- If you don't know a word in English, look it up!

- Teach your class the new words on your poster.

We like reading about ...

dinosaurs

robots

football

B Make word cards for your classroom

- Make some word cards.

- Write the names of things in your classroom. Look in the *Picture dictionary* on page 137.

- Stick each word card on or near the object.

- Teach the words to your class.

- Play 'Please say please'.

Point to the clock, please.

clock

wall

coat pegs

C Introduce your partner

Work with a partner. Ask them some questions.
Write down the answers. Introduce your partner to the class.

What's your name?
How do you spell your name?
How old are you?
What colours do you like?
What do you like reading about?
Have you got any brothers or sisters?

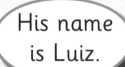

His name is Luiz.

___ name is ___ .

___ is ___ years old.

___ likes the colours ___ and ___ .

___ likes reading about ___ .

___ has got ___ brothers and ___ sisters.

L👀k what I can do!

- I can write about myself.

- I can talk about a book.

- I can name the vowels and read words with short vowel sounds.

- I can say who things belong to.

- I can understand the words of a song.

2 Good neighbours

1 Think about it   Who lives in your neighbourhood?

11 **1 Read and listen**

Look at the picture. Find some neighbours helping neighbours.

> **My neighbourhood**
>
> Come and meet the people in my neighbourhood.
>
> There are neighbours helping neighbours in my neighbourhood.
>
> There are grandmas, grandpas, cousins,
>
> Mums and dads, girls and boys,
>
> In my neighbourhood, the streets around my home.

12 **2 Ben's neighbourhood**

Listen and find Ben in the picture.

Point to what he describes.

Unit 2 Lesson 1 Vocabulary: people **Use of English:** present simple questions and short answer forms **Read/Listen:** *My neighbourhood*; aural comprehension
Talk: asking questions; the family **Write:** guided writing

Listen, point and say. Then listen, look at the big picture and answer the questions.

young people   police officer   nurse   street cleaner   old people

4 💬 Ask questions

Look at the picture. Ask questions beginning with **What? Who?** or **How many?**

What is the police officer doing?

Who is the nurse helping?

How many women can you see?

5 📝 💬 My family

Look at the family tree.
Who are the people in the picture?
Draw and label your family.
Talk about your picture.

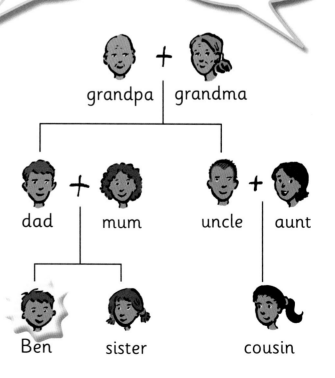

grandpa | grandma

dad   mum   uncle | aunt

Ben   sister   cousin

14 1 A letter from Fiona

Listen and read the letter. Talk about the questions.

Dear everybody,
My name is Fiona Littleton. I am eight years old. I live in an apartment. My family lives on the second floor. Look at my picture. Can you see me?

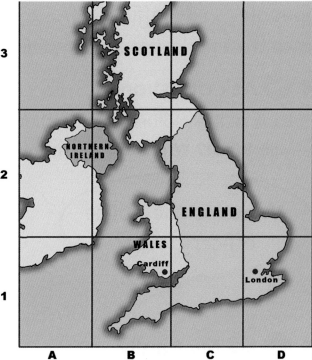

I live in Cardiff. Cardiff is a city in Wales. Wales is a country in the United Kingdom. We call it 'the UK'. On the map, Cardiff is in square B-1. Can you see it?

My grandparents live in a city in square D-1 of the map. Can you find the city?

This is my address.

What's your address?

Maybe we can visit each other some day!
Your friend,
Fiona

Fiona Littleton
Apartment 10
16 Chadwick Street
Cardiff
Wales

2 Continents

Fiona lives in the UK. The UK is in Europe.

Europe is a continent. How many continents are there?

Which one do you live in?

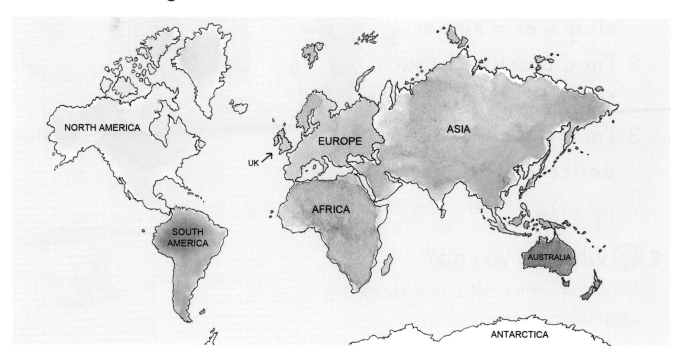

3 In the lift: Going up!

There is a lift in Fiona's apartment building.
She likes pressing the buttons in the lift.
Which button does she press to get
to each floor?

fourth floor   4

second floor

first floor

third floor

4 A letter to Fiona

Write a letter to Fiona. Tell her your name, age and address.

Draw a picture of you in front of your home.

15 1 What is your job?

Listen and repeat the sentences. Listen to the sound that *-er* makes.

1 I'm a **singer**. I sing.

    sing + er = singer

2 I'm a **teacher**. I **teach**.

    teach + er = teacher

3 I'm a **dancer**. I **dance**.

    dance + r = dancer

Would you like to be a singer, a teacher or a dancer?

2 [AB] **What do you do?**

Finish the sentences below by saying
what the person does.

1 I am a **window cleaner**.

    I <u>**clean**</u> windows.

2 I am a **writer**. I ___ books.

3 I am a **painter**. I ___ .

4 I am a **clothes designer**.

    I ___ clothes.

5 I am a **baker**. I ___ bread.

6 I am a **taxi driver**. I ___ a taxi.

7 I am a **street cleaner**.

    I ___ the street.

Are you a singer?

No, I'm not. Try again!

3 💬 **Who am I?**

Act out a worker at work. Your friends ask questions to guess your job.

4 The firefighter

Mr Lucas is a **firefighter**. Listen to find out what a firefighter does. Point to the things he talks about.

fire station

firefighter's uniform

fire engine

ladder

fire alarm

Listen again to answer the questions.

1 Where does Mr Lucas work?

2 What clothes does a firefighter wear?

3 What does Mr Lucas do when the fire alarm rings?

4 What do firefighters use to put out a fire?

5 Why does Mr Lucas go to schools?

5 📝 **Interview your teacher**

Imagine you are a TV reporter and interview your teacher. Use these questions:

What is your job?

Where do you work?

What do you do?

Listen to your teacher's answers. Then write your TV report.

1 At the shopping centre

Look at the map of a shopping centre.

Put your finger on the **red** star.

Go straight ahead.

Which shops are on your right?

Which shops are on your left?

At the end, turn right.

Now which shops are on your left?

Which shop is on your right?

2 📝 Find the mystery shop

Read the clues.

Name each mystery shop.

1 It's **between** the bookshop
and the sweet shop.

2 It's **next to** the sports shop.

3 It's **opposite** the computer shop.

Write a new clue. Read it aloud.
Can your friends find it?

Language tip

next to

between

opposite

17 **3** 💬 **Asking for directions**

Listen and follow the directions.
Practise the conversation with a partner.
Choose a shop and give directions.

Excuse me, where is
the computer shop?

18 4 Behind, between, inside, on, under

Look at the pictures. Then listen and follow the instructions.

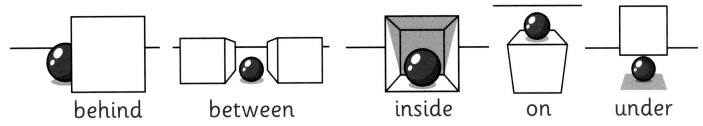

behind   between   inside   on   under

19 5 Find the treasure

Two children are on a treasure hunt. Listen to each clue.

Where do the children look? Where is the treasure?

6 ✎ Make up a clue

Say a clue for your partner.
Your partner must point to the map.

> Look behind the ... .

7 ✎ 📝 Classroom treasure hunt

Work with a group of children. Write four clues for your classroom.
Then hide clues 2 to 4 and give clue 1 to another group!
Here are some examples:

1 Look next to the crayons.

2 Look under the teacher's chair.

4 Look behind the door.

3 Look inside a red book.

Clue 4 leads to the treasure! Where did these children put the treasure?

5 Read and respond

1 Before you read

Read the title of the poem. Do you know another
word that means the same as 'kids'?

A lot of kids

There are a lot of kids

Living in my apartment building

And a lot of apartment buildings on my street

And a lot of streets in this city

And cities in this country

And a lot of countries in the world.

So I wonder if somewhere there's a kid I've never met
Living in some building on some street
In some city and country I'll never know —
And I wonder if that kid and I might be best friends
If we ever met.

Jeff Moss

2 💬 Talk about the poem

1 Where does the girl in this poem live?

2 Are there many apartment buildings on her street?

3 Do you think the girl is **friendly** or **unfriendly**?

4 Do you think this poem is **happy** or **unhappy**?

3 📝 💬 Friends around the world

Pretend you are meeting a new friend from another country.
Choose one of the photos and make up a name card for that child.

Name:

Age:

Country:

Likes:

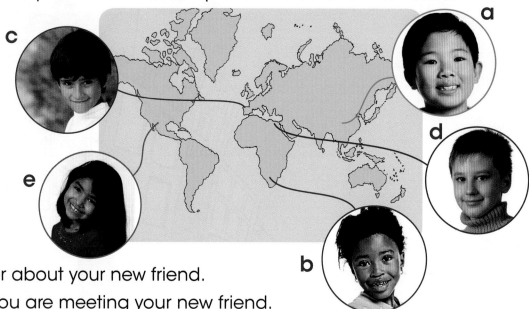

Tell your partner about your new friend.
Then pretend you are meeting your new friend.
Make up a conversation with your partner.

Hi! What's your name?

What's your favourite ...?

Do you like ...?

Let's play!

Where do you live?

Words to remember

Find these words in the poem:
friends some there city.
Practise spelling them.

21 **4** 🎵 **The world is our neighbourhood**

The people who live in our street are our neighbours. People who live in other countries are also our neighbours on Planet Earth. Listen and join in the song.

We've got the whole world in our hands

Chorus We've got the whole world in our hands. (sing 4 times)

We've got our brothers and our sisters in our hands,
We've got our friends and our family in our hands,
We've got people everywhere in our hands,
We've got the whole world in our hands.

We've got the sun and the rain in our hands,
We've got the moon and the stars in our hands,
We've got the wind and the clouds in our hands,
We've got the whole world in our hands.

We've got the rivers and the mountains in our hands,
We've got the seas and the oceans in our hands,
We've got the towns and the cities in our hands,
We've got the whole world in our hands.

town
city

mountain

sea
ocean

river

6 Choose a project Who lives in your neighbourhood?

A Make a book: What can you be when you grow up?

- Think of some interesting jobs. Look in the *Picture dictionary* on page 140.

- Make a page for each job.

- Draw a picture and write a sentence:

  > You can be a ___ .

- Write a second sentence about the work that person does. Some examples are in the picture.

You can be a scientist.
A scientist discovers new things.

You can be an architect.
An architect designs new buildings.

B Do a survey: What do you want to be?

- Make a chart.

- Choose five interesting jobs.

- Ask your classmates:

  ### What do you want to be when you grow up?

- They must write their name on the chart.

- Look at the chart opposite. Which job is the most popular?

Sam	Elsa	Lisa	Farah	Leon
Vijay	Seth			
Maya				
Franco	Nadia	Amir		
Hakim	Basil	Layla	Nina	

c. Draw a school map

- Draw a map of the rooms in your school.

- Label the rooms.

- A visitor comes to your school.

- Put your finger on the **red** star.

- Tell the visitor how to get to: your classroom, the office, another room.

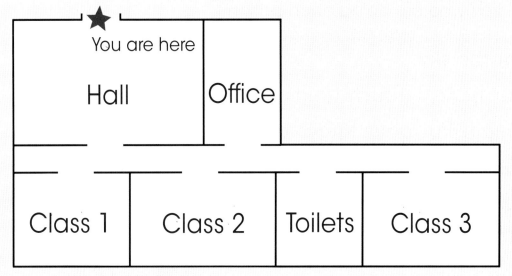

★ You are here Hall	Office		
Class 1	Class 2	Toilets	Class 3

LOOk what I can do!

- I can name people and things in my neighbourhood.

- I can talk about where I live.

- I can talk and write about different jobs.

- I can ask for and give directions.

- I can read and talk about a poem.

Fiona Littleton
Apartment 10
16 Chadwick Street
Cardiff
Wales

1 Think about it — How can we move in different ways?

22 1 Read and listen

Join in and do the actions. Then look at the picture.
Find the children who are doing each action.

Reach for the sky

Clap your hands. Touch your toes.

Turn around. Put your finger on your nose.

Flap your arms. Jump up high.

Wiggle your fingers and reach for the sky!

23 2 'Get up and move' day

Listen to Julia. What are the children doing? Can you wave
your hands and hop on one foot and nod your head?

Listen, point and say.

wave

stand

hop

fall

flap

wiggle

nod

head
nose
arm
tummy
hand
fingers
leg
foot
toes

Touch your tummy.

Take turns giving instructions to your class.
Choose parts of the body.

4 💬 Say it and do it

Give your partner three instructions using one word from each box.
Can your partner do all three actions at the same time?

Clap Wave Shake	your hands.	Tap Hop on Stand on	one foot.	Nod Shake Roll	your head.

Listen carefully. Do the actions as you count.

1 2 3 4 5 6 7 8 9 10
11 12 13 14 15 16 17 18 19 20

2 Find out more What can birds do?

1 🧪 **Before you read**

What do you know about birds? Say five things. Look at the **headings**.
Can all birds fly? Where will you find the answer? Now listen and read.

Amazing birds

Laying eggs

All birds have feathers, and all birds lay eggs.
A hummingbird has the smallest egg. It is as
small as your fingernail. An ostrich has the
biggest egg. It is as big as 24 hen's eggs.

Building nests

Most birds build nests for their eggs, but
some birds don't. Emperor penguins don't
build nests. The father penguin balances
the egg on his feet. His tummy keeps the
egg warm. Some birds lay their eggs on
the ground.

Flying

Most birds can fly, but some birds can't.
An ostrich can't fly, but it can run very fast.
A penguin can't fly, but it can swim very fast.

Swimming

Ducks and swans can swim. They can fly too!

Unit 3 Lesson 2 Use of English: *can/can't* for ability; pronouns: *it, they*; conjunctions: *and, but, or*; determiners: *all, most, some* **Read:** *Amazing birds*
Write: information from a chart

2 🗫 Talk about it

What new facts did you learn?

Which of these birds live near you?

3 True or false?

Look at the text *Amazing birds*. Is each statement **true** or **false**?

1 Most birds build nests.

2 Some birds can swim.

3 A penguin can fly, but it can't swim.

4 A duck can swim and fly.

5 An ostrich can fly.

4 All, most, some

Finish these sentences. How many different sentences can you make?

All birds ____

Most birds ____

Some birds ____

Language tip

and   but   or

I can run **and** jump.

I can walk, **but** I can't fly.

A bird can't read **or** ride a bike.

5 📝 What can birds do?

Say what the birds below **can** and **can't** do.

Write a sentence about each bird.

	fly	swim	walk
kiwi			✔
hummingbird	✔		
goose	✔	✔	✔
falcon	✔		✔

A kiwi can't fly **or** swim, **but** it can walk.

3 Words and sounds Long vowel sounds

27 1 Which vowel sound?

A long vowel sound says the name of the vowel: **a e i o u**.
Write the vowels **a**, **i** and **o** on three pieces of paper.
Listen for the sound in the middle of these words.
Hold up the vowel sound you hear.

28 2 🗨 Silent e

Listen and say the word pairs.
How does the silent **e** change
the sound of the vowel?

Tim   time
Sam   same

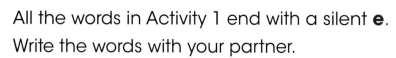

Look! Sam is the same as Tim!

All the words in Activity 1 end with a silent **e**.
Write the words with your partner.

29 3 🗨 Revision of ai and ay

Read and find three words with a long **a** sound.
Listen to check. What letters make this sound?

Mr Gray: Let's wait for the train. Stay away from the wet paint!

Daisy Gray: There's a snail on the railway. I hate snails. I hate
rainy days.

Mr Gray: Here comes the train. Move away, Snail!

Unit 3 Lesson 3 Use of English: adjectives to express feelings **Phonics:** long vowels with silent *e*; long *a* diphthongs *ai* and *ay* **Song:** *If you're happy and you know it*
Talk: feelings

4 💬 How are you feeling?

scared   tired   unhappy   cross   puzzled   excited

Look at the photos. Act out a word for your partner to guess.

Are you feeling scared?

No, I'm not. Try again!

surprised   hungry

30 5 🎵 Sing about it

Listen to the song. Join in and do the actions.

If you're happy and you know it

If you're **happy** and you know it, **clap** your hands.

If you're **happy** and you know it, **clap** your hands.

If you're **happy** and you know it,

And you really want to show it,

If you're **happy** and you know it, **clap** your hands.

Make up some new verses. Choose words to fill in the spaces. Sing your new verses!

Hurray!

If you're **excited** and you know it, **shout 'Hurray!'**

If you're **tired** and you know it, **you can sleep**.

If you're **scared** and you know it, …

If you're **unhappy** and you know it, …

If you're **hungry** and you know it, …

4 Use of English — Revision of *-ing* forms

1 What can you do with a piece of paper?

Read each sentence and act it out. Don't use real paper!

1  I'm waving it.

2 You're ripping it.

3  He's cutting it.

4 She's folding it.

We're writing on it.

5

6  They're making a ball with it.

2 🗨 Listen and guess

Sit back to back with your partner.
A: Do something with a piece of paper.
B: Listen carefully. Guess what your partner is doing.

Partner A   Partner B

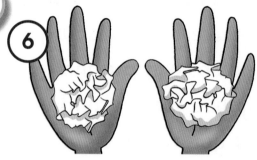

Are you cutting the paper?

No, I'm not. Try again.

Unit 3 Lesson 4 Use of English: present continuous; spelling rules when adding *-ing*; *I like / don't like* + verb + *-ing*; conjunctions: *and, or* Talk: guessing actions; likes Write: likes and dislikes

3 📝 What do you like doing?

Look at the activities below. Write what you like. Write what you *don't* like.

swimming   using a computer

watching TV   shopping

skipping   playing football

eating ice cream   riding a bike

I like swimming, shopping and skipping.
I don't like riding a bike or watching TV.

4 📝 💬 Interview your partner

Ask your partner what he or she likes.

Do you like swimming?

Write two sentences.

Cora likes swimming and eating ice cream.
She doesn't like playing football or shopping.

5 Read and respond

1 Before you read

The characters in this play are talking animals.
There is also a **narrator** who helps tell the story.
Look at the pictures. What animal characters are in this play?

> **About the story**
>
> This story is from the Seneca Indians in the United States.

Bear and Turtle have a race

Narrator: One cold winter day, Bear was walking and singing.

Bear: I'm the best in the forest. I'm the fastest runner of all. I'm big and fast and strong and brave! I'm the very best bear of all.

Turtle 1: Bear is always boasting!

Turtle 2: I think we need to teach him a lesson.

Narrator: The turtles whispered together. They had a plan.

Turtle 2: Good idea!

Turtle 3: Very clever.

Turtle 4: Let's do it!

Narrator: The next day, Bear saw Turtle sitting on a rock.

Bear: What are you doing, Turtle?

Turtle 1: I'm writing a song:
'I'm the best in the forest.
I'm the fastest swimmer of all …'

Bear: That is a silly song!
Bears are fast. Turtles are slow.

Turtle 1: Not when we are swimming.
I can swim faster than you can run.

Bear: That is ridiculous. Let's have a race.

Turtle 1: OK! Let's meet at the pond tomorrow.
I can swim, you can run.

Narrator: The animals came to watch the race.

Rabbit and Frog: We're cheering for Turtle.

Deer and Fox: We're cheering for Bear.

Crow: Ready, steady, go!

Turtle 4: Hurry up, Bear! I'm going faster than you.

Bear: Wow! That turtle is swimming fast!

Turtle 3: Hurry up, Bear!

Bear: I'm running as fast as I can.

Turtle 2: Hurry up, Bear. I'm winning.

Bear: Oh no, I'm losing the race.

Crow: Turtle is the winner!

Deer and Fox: Turtle's won the race!

Rabbit and Frog: Hooray for Turtle!

Bear: I'm going to my cave.
I don't want to see anyone.
I'm going to sleep all winter.

Narrator: When everyone had gone, Turtle knocked on the ice three times.

Turtle 1: You can come out now.

Turtles 2, 3 and 4: We did it!

Turtle 2: Yes. Turtles are not fast, but we are clever!

2 💬 **Talk about it**

1 Why do the turtles want to teach Bear a lesson?
2 Which animals come to watch the race?
3 What does Crow say to start the race?
4 How does Bear feel at the end of the race?

excited   tired   puzzled   happy   unhappy   cross

5 How does Turtle feel at the end of the race?

excited   tired   puzzled   happy   unhappy   cross

6 How many turtles were really in the race?
7 Do you think the race was fair or unfair?

3 💬 **Act out the play**

Work with a group of friends. Have fun!

6 Choose a project — How can we move in different ways?

A Lead an action game

- Learn these five body words. (Look in the *Picture dictionary* on page 135.)

  elbow   knee   wrist   ankle   shoulder

- Choose five more body words.
  Write all the words on cards.

- Play a game with your class.
  Pick two cards. Say the words as
  you ask the question:

  **Can you put your elbow
  on your ear?**

  Your classmates will try! They will say
  Yes, we can! or No, we can't!

B Write an animal riddle: Who am I?

I am small and slow.

I like walking, swimming and eating bugs.

You can find me on a rock or in a pond.

Look at this riddle. Can you guess the answer?

Write your own animal riddles!

I am __ and __ .
I like __ , __ and __ .
You can find me __ or __ .

> I am small and slow.
>
> I like walking, swimming and eating bugs.
>
> You can find me on a rock or in a pond.
>
> Who am I?

Answer: A turtle.

C Make a counting book: Frog maths

- Make a maths book about frogs, with 10 pages.

  The first page has 1 frog. The second page has 2 frogs …
  The last page has 10 frogs.

1 frog
2 eyes
4 legs

2 frogs
4 eyes
___ legs

How many legs do 2 frogs have?

- Make a cover for your book. Write the title and authors on the cover.

L**oo**k what I can do!

- I can use action words to give instructions.

- I can talk about birds and what they can and can't do.

- I can read and write words with long vowel sounds.

- I can say what I like and don't like doing.

- I can read, talk about and act out a play script.

4 The big sky

1 Think about it   What is the sky like?

32 **1 Read and listen**

Can you see your shadow now? Jump. Does your shadow jump too?

> **My shadow**
>
> I have a little shadow that goes in and out with me,
> And what can be the use of him is more than I can see.
> He is very, very like me from the heels up to the head;
> And I see him jump before me, when I jump into my bed.
>
> **Robert Louis Stevenson**

in the morning

at midday

in the afternoon

33 **2** 🖼 **Looking at shadows**

Sally is talking to her mother. Listen and point to the right pictures.

Listen, point and say. Then look outside and answer the questions.

long

short

sky   sun   cloud   shadow   short

4 💬 Talk about the pictures

Sally is talking to her mum **in the afternoon**.

1 Is her shadow long or short?   Her shadow **is** ___ .

2 Is the weather sunny or cloudy?   The weather **is** ___ .

Sally looked at her shadow **in the morning**.

3 Was her shadow long or short?   Her shadow **was** ___ .

4 In the morning, was the weather
sunny or cloudy?   The weather **was** ___ .

5 And **at midday**?

5 🧪 Make a sundial

Follow these instructions.

1 Roll a piece of clay into a ball.

2 Put the clay on a plate.

3 Push a straw into the clay.

4 Leave your sundial in a sunny place.

5 Look at the shadow and watch how it moves.

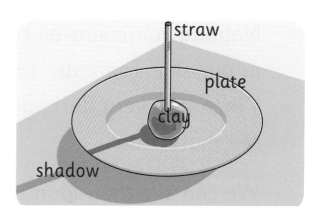

straw

plate

clay

shadow

1 **Before you read**

Do you know the answers to these questions? Read to find out.

Can we see the Sun in the day or at night?

What are clouds made of?

Can we see stars in the day?

What can we see in the sky by day?
The Sun and clouds

In the day, we can see the Sun. The Sun
is a star. It's the nearest star to our planet,
Earth. It is the only star we can see in the day.

Clouds are made of lots of tiny drops of water.
Water comes down from the clouds as rain or snow.

What can we see in the sky at night?
The Moon and stars

Nobody can count all the stars
in our sky. There are too many.
When it is very dark, you can
see more stars.

We can see the Moon because the Sun shines light on it.
Sometimes we see a whole round Moon, and sometimes we
see only part of the Moon.

Why do we have day and night?

The Sun shines on our planet, Earth. Earth turns round slowly. So half of our planet is light and half of our planet is dark. When it is light, we have day. When it is dark, we have night.

Sun

Sunlight

Earth

Try it out!

You need:

A torch (Sun)

A ball (Earth).

1 Put a sticker on Earth where you live.

2 Shine the torch on the ball.

3 Turn the ball around slowly.

4 When the sticker faces the sun, it is day.

5 When the sticker is turned away, it is night.

2  **Write about it**

With your partner, say an interesting fact about:

the sun   clouds   stars   the moon.

Draw a picture and write one sentence for each.

37 **1 Words with the long i sound**

Find the words with each different ending: *-ite*, *-ine*, *-ight*.

bite line   shine   night   right   kite

Which words above rhyme with **bite**?

How do you spell the three words?:

a    **b**   **c**

38 **2 Spelling dictation**

Listen to the spelling and write the word.
Point to the picture above. Say the word.

39 **3 Poem**

Read the poem. Sailors sometimes look at the
sky to find out what the weather will be like.

> Red sky at night,
> Sailor's delight.
> Red sky in the morning,
> Sailor's warning.

Which words rhyme?
Which words have the long **i** sound?
Which letter makes the long **i** sound in **sky**?

4 Compound words

A **compound** word is a big word made of two little words.
Find the two little words in each big word.
How many syllables are there in each word?
Clap the syllables.

sunshine = sun + shine 2

1 sunlight   **4** night-time

2 moonlight   **5** nightclothes

3 daytime   **6** daylight

Choose a word for each clue:

a The light from the sun.

b The opposite of daytime.

c The opposite of night-time.

d Clothes that you wear in bed.

At night-time, Tom looked at the moonlight in his nightclothes.

5 

5 Time expressions

Where were you yesterday?
Ask your partner questions.
Use the time expressions in the box.

Where were you in the morning?

I was at school.

Then ask about another person in the family.

Where was your little sister in the afternoon?

She was at home.

Language tip

in the morning

in the afternoon

in the evening

at night

40 **1 Listen and talk**

Listen to the poem. Join in and do the actions.

We travelled by spaceship

We **travelled** by spaceship to outer space.
Far, far away. We were very brave.
  We **waved** at the Earth.
  We **watched** the Earth get smaller and smaller.

We travelled by spaceship to outer space.
Far, far away. We were very brave.
  We jumped out of the spaceship.
  We walked on the Moon.

We travelled by spaceship to outer space.
Far, far away. We were very brave.
  We climbed back into the spaceship.
  We travelled home.

We travelled by spaceship to outer space.
Far, far away. We were very brave.

2 Verbs ending in -ed

Find all the verbs – the words that tell us what the children did. The first ones are in **red**. Find some more. They end in **-ed**.

Language detective

Can you find a compound word in the poem?

41 3 📝 💬 **We travelled by submarine**

Use these verbs to fill in the gaps in a new poem. You can use each verb once. Then listen to check.

watched   travelled   talked

~~climbed~~   waved   walked

We ¹__ by submarine to the bottom of the sea.

We ²__ at the ship.

We ³ climbed out of the submarine.

We ⁴__ on the bottom of the sea.

We ⁵__ the fishes.

We ⁶__ to an octopus.

Then we travelled back home.

Hello!

4 📝 💬 **What did you do yesterday?**

Interview your partner. Choose words from the *Word box*.

What did you do yesterday?

I walked to the park and I **played** with my sister.

Then write what your partner did.
Write the name of the day (yesterday).

Word box

watched TV

used a computer

helped (who?)

played (what?)

walked (where?)

talked to (who?)

brushed
(my hair? my teeth?)

Tuesday
Peng walked to the park and he played with his sister.

5 Read and respond

1 🧪 **Before you read**

You are going to find out how people learned about the sky many years ago. The people came from Egypt, Mexico, Greece, China and Italy. Find these countries on the map.

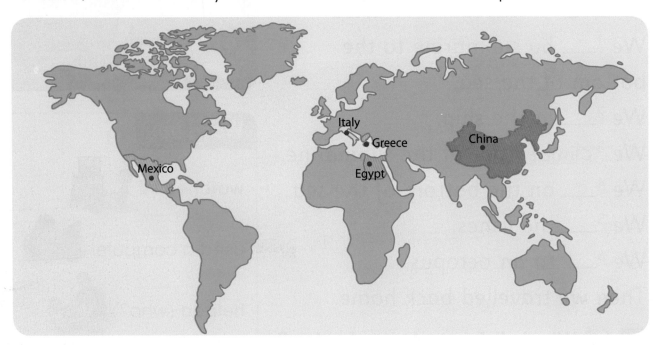

Astronomers all over the world

An astronomer is a person who studies the stars and planets. Today, astronomers look at the sky with big, powerful telescopes. They can take photos of the planets with cameras.

Many, many years ago, astronomers didn't have telescopes or cameras. But they watched the sky and they **learned** many new things.

A photo of the planet Mars

Ancient Egypt

The people of ancient Egypt learned to tell the time by looking at the stars. One very famous astronomer was Hypatia of Alexandria. She **lived** in Egypt two thousand years ago. She **wrote** books about maths and astronomy.

Hypatia of Alexandria

The Mayan people in Mexico

The Mayan people lived mainly in Mexico. Mayan astronomers **made** special buildings to watch the stars and planets in the sky. They learned how the planets move. They measured light and shadows. The Mayans **thought** that the Earth was flat.

Observatory at Chichen Itza, Mexico

Ancient Greece

The people of ancient Greece learned that the Earth goes round the Sun. They **gave** names to many of the planets. The word **planet** is from a Greek word.

Ancient China

The people of China learned a lot about the night sky. They **knew** that the Moon is round. They knew that the Sun shines light on the Moon.

Ancient Rome

The people of ancient Rome (in Italy today) learned many important things. They learned that the Earth goes round the Sun in one year. They learned that the Moon goes round the Earth in one month. They made a calendar. Their calendar was similar to our calendar today.

Words to remember

Find these words in the story:

many people about.

Practise spelling them.

Unit 4 Lesson 5 Read: *Astronomers all over the world;* matching verbs; true/false questions **Use of English:** past simple verbs (regular and irregular)
Talk: describing a picture

2 True or false?

Look at the texts. Is each statement **true** or **false**?

1 An astronomer is a person who looks at animals.

2 We can use a telescope to look at the planets.

3 Hypatia wrote books about birds.

4 The Mayans thought that the Earth was round.

5 The people of ancient Greece gave names to many planets.

6 The people of ancient Rome made a calendar.

3 Match the verbs

Match the verbs in the past with the verbs in the present.
Can you find them in the texts in **red**?

past	present
learned	think
lived	live
wrote	learn
made	write
thought	know
gave	give
knew	make

4 Spot the difference

Look at the two pictures with your partner. Take turns to say one thing which is different. How many differences did you find?

A Make a game: What did you do yesterday?

- Make word cards. On each card write a past tense verb. Draw a picture.

- Then make four time cards: write **yesterday**, **last night**, **in the morning** and **in the afternoon**.

- Play the game with your class. Take a verb card and a time card. Can your classmates make up a sentence with those words in?

What did you do last night?

I played in my bedroom.

B Make a cloud-shaped book

- Cut out a picture of a cloud.

- Trace the cloud picture on pieces of paper. Make them into a book.

- On each page, write a sentence about the sky.

- On the cover, write the name of the book and the authors.

There are white clouds in the sky

At night there are stars

C Write a poem: We travelled by plane

- Think of an exciting place to travel to. Write a poem.
  You can use words from the box:

looked at	waved
travelled	walked
talked	jumped
climbed	

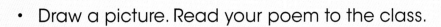

- Draw a picture. Read your poem to the class.

> We travelled by plane to Antarctica.
> We jumped in the snow.
> We waved to the penguins.

L👀k what I can do!

- I can use **is** and **was**.

- I can talk about the sky.

- I can read and write words with the long **i** sound.

- I can say what I did yesterday.

- I can read and talk about an information text.

5 Let's count and measure

1 Think about it How do we use numbers?

43 **1** [1+2] 🎵 **Read and listen**

Find the children in the picture who are singing this song.
Sing and join in the actions. You need 10 children!

> **100 little fingers**
>
> 10 little, 20 little, 30 little fingers.
> 40 little, 50 little, 60 little fingers.
> 70 little, 80 little, 90 little fingers.
> 100 little fingers in the air!

Jack 60 cm
Maria 48 cm
Liz 72 cm

44 **2** [1+2] **A maths lesson**

The children in Class 2 are having a maths lesson.
They are using numbers to count, measure and tell
the time. Listen and point to the children you hear.

Unit 5 Lesson 1 Vocabulary: numbers to 100; *How many? How far …? What time is it? +* time to the hour **Read/Listen:** *100 little fingers;* aural comprehension
Talk: the time

Listen, point and say.

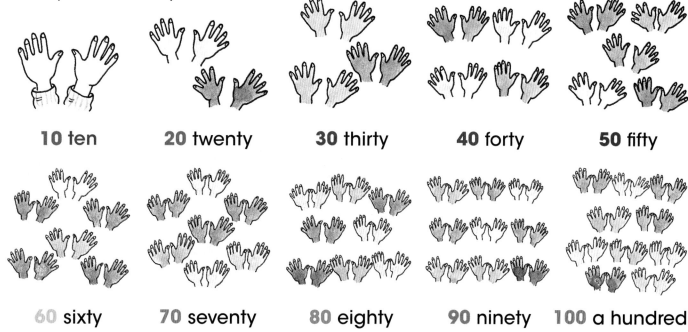

| **10** ten | **20** twenty | **30** thirty | **40** forty | **50** fifty |

| **60** sixty | **70** seventy | **80** eighty | **90** ninety | **100** a hundred |

Listen and count from 20 to 30.

20 21 **22** 23 **24** 25 **26** 27 28 **29** **30**

Clap your hands and count from 30 to 100.

46 **4** [1+2] **How far can you jump?**

Listen again. How far did Carlos jump?
Measure how far you can jump.
Write it on a piece of paper.
Put the papers in order from smallest to biggest.

Language tip

The letters **cm** stand for the word **centimetre**.

5 💬 [1+2] **What time is it?**

Point to a clock. Ask your partner the time.

What time is it?

It's two o'clock.

1 [1+2] **Before you read**

What do we use to measure things? Find out how people measured things many years ago.

Measuring in ancient Egypt

Long ago in Egypt, people measured with their fingers, hands and arms.

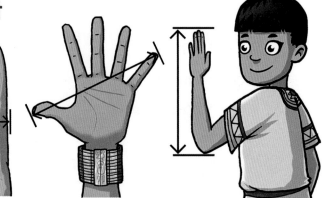

Try it out!

How many **fingers** long is this line? _____

How many **hands** long is your book?

How many **arms** long is your table?

Measuring in ancient Rome

Long ago in Rome, people measured in **footsteps**.

Try it out!

Measure your classroom in footsteps.

How many footsteps long is it?

Ask your teacher to measure your classroom in footsteps.

Is your teacher's answer the same as your answer? Why not?

Measuring today

Today we use the metric system to measure.

We use centimetres and metres.

There are 100 centimetres in a metre.

This line is 1 centimetre long. ▬

2 [1+2] Centimetres or metres?

We use **centimetres** to measure small things.

We use **metres** to measure big things.

What would you use to measure these things?

 Your school hall   centimetres   metres

 A leaf   centimetres   metres

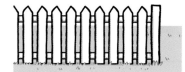 A fence   centimetres   metres

3 [💬] [1+2] How long is it?

Use a ruler to measure these pictures.

a a **paperclip**

How long is it?

It's **3 cm** long.

b a **fish**

c a **shell**

 d a child's **paint brush**

47 **1** Words that sound the same

Some words sound the same,
but have different spellings:

one and **won**

two and **too**

Read and listen to the poem.
Find the words that sound the same.

One-one was a race horse.

Two-two was one too.

One-one won one race.

Two-two won one too.

I won one prize.

I won two prizes

I won two too!

eight and **ate**

The monkey ate eight bananas.

Fill in the missing words to make a tongue twister.

Ed __ __ eggs every day.

Language detective

How many eggs did
Ed eat in a week?

48 **2** Counting in twos

We can count up in twos. Add two more each time. Listen and join in.
Listen and say the poem. Make up a new verse starting with **22**.

2, 4, 6, 8, Mary's at the cottage gate.

Eating cherries on a plate – 2, 4, 6, 8.

49 3 💬 **What an amazing animal!**

We sometimes say **What a … !** when we are surprised or excited.
Listen to these sentences. Say them. Try to sound surprised.

> What a big animal!

Match the sentences with the animals.
Then listen to check.

1 The blue whale is the biggest animal
on Earth. It is about 30 metres long.
That's as long as two buses parked
end to end.
What a ___ !

2 A parrot can learn to talk. It can
count, name colours and do maths.
What a ___ !

3 An African elephant weighs the
same as 100 men.
What a ___ !

4 A very good runner can run 12 metres
in a second. A cheetah can run 30 metres
in a second.
What a ___ !

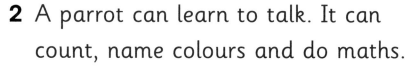

1 Morena's breakfast

This morning, Morena was hungry.
This was her breakfast:

milk   bread

We can count grapes and eggs,
so we say: **some grapes   two eggs**.
We can't count bread, juice or milk,
so we say: **some bread   some juice   some milk   NOT some milks**.

grapes   eggs   orange juice

At breakfast this morning, what did Morena eat? What did she drink?

What did you eat
for breakfast?
What did you drink?

> She ate **two** eggs, **some** bread and **some** grapes.

> She drank **some** juice and **some** milk.

2 The food shop

Look at this shop.
Which foods can you count?
Which can't you count?

3 🗩 Play *I went to the shop*

Play the game. Add one
thing each time.

Player 1: I went to the shop
and I bought **some** orange juice.

Player 2: I went to the shop
and I bought **some** orange juice and **six** carrots.

How many foods can you add to the list?

4 💬 🔢 **A maths story from India**

Birbal was a wise man who lived in India many years ago.
When King Akbar gave him tricky problems to solve, he
always found an answer!
Read the story. What is the problem in this story? What is Birbal's answer?

Clever Birbal

One day, King Akbar picked up a
piece of chalk and drew a line on
the floor. 'Birbal,' he said to his
friend, 'I want you to make this
line shorter. But you mustn't rub
out the ends of the line.'

Birbal looked at the line and thought.
Then he drew a long line under
King Akbar's line. 'Look,' said Birbal.
'My line is longer than your line.
So your line is shorter!'

King Akbar laughed. 'You are right, Birbal,' he said.
'You made my line shorter. What a clever answer!'

Act out the story with a partner. Draw the lines on some paper.

5 📝 **Verbs in the story**

In the story, find the words that are the past simple of:

look   think   draw   laugh   make   say.

Choose four of the words. Write things that you or your family did this morning.

My mother made my breakfast for me.

51 **1** **Before you read**

This is a story about a clever animal.
Read and listen as far as the bottom of page 71,
then stop and think. What will happen next?

Many ways to count to ten

A long time ago, Leopard was the king of the forest.
One day he said, 'I'm getting old and tired.
It's time to choose a new king.'
He put up signs in the forest.

All the animals came to the contest.
King Leopard said, 'Thank you for
coming. Let me explain the contest.
You must throw this spear high into
the air and quickly count to ten.
You must say "ten" before the spear
hits the ground. The winner of the
contest will be the new king of the forest.'

*Contest
Tomorrow
at
3 o'clock*

The elephant was the first to try.
'I'm very big,' he said. 'I think I can do it.'
The elephant threw the spear high into the air.
'1, 2, 3, 4, 5, …,' he counted loudly. Boom!
The spear hit the ground.

I'm sorry, Elephant,' said the king.
'You didn't do it. You didn't count to ten.'

The water ox was second.
'I'm very strong,' he said.
'I think I can do it.'
The water ox threw the spear
high into the air.
'1, 2, 3, 4, 5, 6,' he counted loudly.
Boom! The spear hit the ground.
'I'm sorry, Water Ox,' said the king.
'You didn't do it. You didn't count to ten.'

The chimpanzee was third.
'I can count very quickly,'
he said. 'I think I can do it.'
The chimpanzee threw the
spear high into the air.
'1, 2, 3, 4, 5, 6, 7, 8,'
he counted quickly. Boom!
The spear hit the ground.
'I'm sorry, Chimpanzee,' said the king.
'You didn't do it. You didn't count to ten.'

The little antelope was next.

'Hello, King Leopard,' he said quietly.

'Can I try?'

'Of course, little friend,' said the king.

'Here is the spear.'

The tiny antelope jumped high in the
air as he threw the spear.

'2, 4, 6, 8, 10!' counted the antelope. Boom!

The spear hit the ground.

'You did it!' said the king. 'Well done, Little Antelope!
You counted to ten in twos. What a clever idea!
The forest has a new and very clever king!'

'Three cheers for King Antelope,'
cried the animals.

'Hip, hip, hooray! Hip, hip, hooray!
Hip, hip, hooray!'

 Unit 5 Lesson 5 Read/Talk: *Many ways to count to ten;* comprehension **Vocabulary:** adverbs: *loudly, quickly, quietly;* sight words **Talk:** character voices

2 💬 Talk about it

1 Who are the characters in this story?
2 Where does the story take place?
3 Why did King Leopard want to choose a new king?
4 Which animals speak loudly?
5 Which animal speaks quickly?
6 Which of these words describe the antelope?

   big   strong   tiny   clever   loud   quiet

7 What was the antelope's clever idea?
8 Do you think Little Antelope will be a good king? Why or why not?

3 Who says it?

Match the words with the character.

1 'I'm getting old and tired.'
2 'I can count very quickly.'
3 'I'm very big.'
4 'I'm very strong.'
5 '2, 4, 6, 8, 10!'

> ### Language tip
> The words inside speech marks are the words a character says.
> 'I'm very strong,' he said.

4 💬 Read the characters' words

Your teacher will read the words outside the speech marks.

You will read the characters' words inside the speech marks.

Use different voices for the different characters.

> ### Words to remember
> Find these words in the story:
> was   said   first   new.
> Practise spelling them.

A Make a picture with 100 objects

- You will need coloured paper, scissors and glue.

- Cut out 10 sets of shapes.

  For example:

10 **red** squares	10 **yellow** triangles
10 **blue** squares	10 **red** rectangles
10 **yellow** squares	10 **blue** rectangles
10 **red** triangles	10 **red** hearts
10 **blue** triangles	10 **blue** hearts.

- Use the shapes to make a picture.

- Write three questions about your picture, for example:

  > How many **triangles** are in our picture?
  > How many **blue shapes** are in our picture?
  > How many **red hearts** are in our picture?

B Have a contest

- Choose a contest:

  – How far can you count in English in 30 seconds?

  – How many times can you hop in 30 seconds?

  – How many times can you write your name in 30 seconds?

- Time each person.

> How far can you count in 30 seconds?
> Myriam 33
> Nadia 15
> Hala 26

c Make a measuring book

- Think of 6 questions. For example:

> How long is a new pencil?
>
> How long is Huang's hand?
>
> How tall is the teacher's chair?

How long is
Huang's hand?

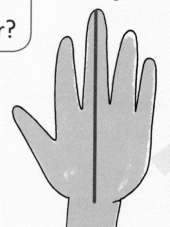

11cm

- Write each question on a page.
  Measure the object. Write the answer.

- Make a flap to cover the answer.

- Your class must try to estimate
  the answer.

L👀k what I can do!

- I can count and read numbers to 100.

- I can measure and say how long something is.

- I can recognise words that sound the same,
  like **one/won** and **two/too**.

- I can say and write what I did this morning.

- I can read, discuss and act out a story.

1 Think about it How are bugs special?

52 **1 Read and listen**

Listen and read the poem. Act it out.

> **The bug**
> One, two, three!
> There's a bug on me.
> Where did it go?
> I don't know.

53 **2 What lives in your garden?**

Listen and point to the animals. Which ones are not talked about?

Do you have these in your country?

3 Topic vocabulary

Listen, say and point. Say where each thing is. Answer the questions.

ant   bee   butterfly   cricket   spider   web

4 🧪 What do you know about insects?

Say what you know about insects. Then listen and answer.

How many legs does an insect have?

Do all insects have wings?

Is a spider an insect?

wings

antennae

5 📝 Write about it

What new information did you learn?
Finish these sentences.

All insects have ___ .

Some insects have ___ .

___ insects have antennae.

legs

> It has two legs.
> It is not an insect.

6 💬 Find the animal

Look at the big picture. Describe an animal.
Can your partner find it?

> It is blue.
> It has six legs.

56 **1** 🔬 **Before you read**

Look at the headings in *Ants* and *Spiders*. How are the headings similar?
What do you think you will learn about?

Ants

What does an ant look like?

An ant is an insect. It has six legs
and two antennae. Ants use their
antennae to feel, smell and taste.
These ants are using their antennae
to communicate. What do you think they are saying?

Where do ants live?

Ants live in big groups.
Some ants build homes with
many rooms under the ground.

What do ants eat?

Ants eat leaves, seeds, bugs and other things.
When ants go to find food, they leave a smell trail.
They carry their food home, following their smell trail.

2 💬 **What can you remember?**

Close your book. Tell your partner some facts you remember
about ants. Then open the book. Read *Ants* again with your partner.
Find some more facts.

3 🖼 **Interesting facts**

Listen and read about spiders. What is the most interesting fact?

Spiders

What does a spider look like?

Spiders are not insects.

All spiders have eight legs.

They don't have antennae or wings.

Some spiders have eight eyes and some have six.

But most spiders can't see very well!

Where do spiders live?

Some spiders live under the ground.

Others make webs. A spider makes

a web from silk in its body.

The silk is very light and very strong.

What do spiders eat?

Most spiders eat insects. Some very

big spiders eat mice and small fish too.

4 📝 AB **Compare insects and spiders**

How are ants and spiders similar? How are they different?

5 📝 **My very own bug: Draw, write and share**

Make up a bug. Draw a picture. Give it a name.

Where does your bug live?

What does it eat?

What can it do?

3 Words and sounds — Rhyming words, long e

1 Find the rhyming word

Read the pairs of sentences below. Each missing word rhymes with the word in **red**. Where is the cricket? Use words from the picture.

1 Oh no, oh **no**!

There's a cricket on my ___ .

2 Oh poor, poor **me**!

There's a cricket on my ___ .

3 Oh this cricket's such a **pest**!

Now it's sitting on my ___ .

4 Did you hear what I **said**?

There's a cricket on my ___ .

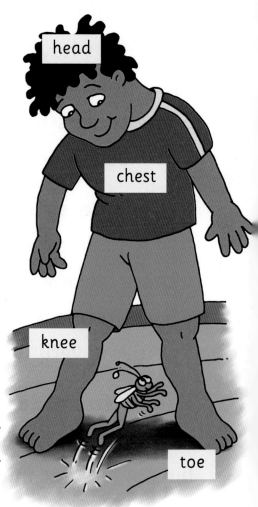

58 2 🎵 Listen and sing

Listen and join in. Point to where the cricket is.

A cricket on the floor

There's a cricket on the floor, on the floor.
There's a cricket on the floor, on the floor.
Now it's coming through the door,
That cricket on the floor.
There's a cricket on the floor, on the floor.

Now the cricket's on my **toe**, on my **toe**.

Now the cricket's on my **knee**, on my **knee**.

Now the cricket's on my **chest**, on my **chest**.

Now the cricket's on my **head**, on my **head**.
Now there's a cricket on the floor, on the floor.

3 💬 Long e spellings **ea** and **ee**

Say these words. What vowel sound do they all have?

knee   flea   me   bee   she   leaf   feet   eat

Write the words. Underline the letters that stand for the long **e** sound.

Do a spelling quiz with your partner.
Ask your partner to spell three words.
Then your partner will ask you three words.

How do you spell **bee**?

B - e - e

I'm a flea!

4 📝 💬 **Same letters, different sound!**

Sometimes **ea** makes a different sound.
How do you say these words?

head   weather

Listen to the poem. Which words have the long **e** sound? Which words have the short **e** sound?

A bee and a flea
Had breakfast with tea.
The bee bumped his head
And went back to bed.

Make a chart. Write the words with the long **e** sound on one side and with the short **e** on the other side.

long **e** sound	short **e** sound

4 Use of English   Writing questions

1 📝 💬 Ask and answer

Read the information about **bees**. Then read the question.
What is the answer?

> **Bees** are helpful insects. They make honey.
> People like eating honey.
> ***Question:*** How do bees help people?

Now read about **silkworms**. Complete the question.
What is the answer?

> **Silkworms** are helpful insects. They make
> silk. People use silk to make beautiful clothes.
> ***Question:*** How ___ help people?

Now do the same with **crickets** and **butterflies**.

> **A cricket** hasn't got ears. It hears
> sounds through special spots on its legs.
> ***Question:*** How does a cricket ___ ?

> **A butterfly** hasn't got a mouth.
> It tastes food with its feet.
> ***Question:*** How does ... ?

2 💬 📝 Prepare a game: All about bugs

1 You are going to write questions for a game. You are A or B.

   A: Look at **Ants** on page 78.

   B: Look at **Spiders** on page 79.

2 Write four questions starting with:

Does ... ?   What does ... ?   How does ... ?   How many ... ?

Do ... ?   What do ... ?   How do ... ?   How many ... ?

3 Write each question on a card.

4 On the back of the card, draw 1 star ⭐ for an easy question or 2 stars ⭐⭐ for a hard question.

5 Give your cards to your teacher.

3 Play 'All about bugs'

Follow the instructions.

How to play

- Play in two teams.
- Teams take turns to choose an **easy** or **hard** question.
- You score like this:

   2 points for a hard question

   1 point for an easy question

   0 points for a wrong answer.

Language tip

One bug
What does a bug eat?

Lots of bugs
What do bugs eat?

The bug game

Team 1

Team 2

60 1 Before you read

Look at the pictures. Who are the characters in this story?
What do you think happens? Now read the story.

Little Ant

It was autumn. The weather was getting cold.
Little Ant said, 'I'm going outside to play'.

'Come home soon,' said Little Ant's mother.
'It's getting cold outside. But our home
under the ground is nice and warm.'

Little Ant met a beetle and a worm.
'Hello,' said Little Ant. 'Let's play!'
'OK,' said the beetle and the worm.
They played and played together.

The wind began to **blow**. Little Ant began to **shiver**.
'It's cold,' she said. 'I have to go home.'

Little Ant started to walk home.
The wind blew harder and Little Ant shivered.
A big leaf fell on her.
'Help!' said Little Ant. 'I can't move!'

'Leaf, please get off me,' said Little Ant.
'I have to go home.'
But the leaf didn't move.

Little Ant called to a mouse.
'Mouse, Mouse! I need help.
Please **lift up** the leaf.
It's cold and I have to go home.'

But the mouse said, 'Sorry, Little Ant.
I haven't got time to help.
I'm very busy.'

So Little Ant called to a cat.
'Cat, Cat! I need help.
Please **chase** the mouse.
Mouse, please lift up the leaf.
It's cold and I have to go home.'

But the cat said, 'Sorry, Little Ant.
I haven't got time to help.
I'm very busy.'

So Little Ant called to a dog.
'Dog, Dog! I need help.
Please **scare** the cat.
Cat, please chase the mouse.
Mouse, please lift up the leaf.
It's cold and I have to go home.'

But the dog said, 'Sorry, Little Ant.
I haven't got time to help.
I'm very busy.'

A flea who lived on the dog
heard Little Ant calling for help.
The flea is a cousin of the ant.

'Don't worry, Cousin Ant,' called the flea.
'I can help. I'll **bite** this dog.'
So the flea bit the dog.

The dog yelped and scared the cat.

The cat turned and chased the mouse.

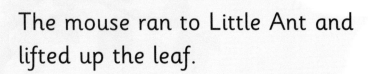

The mouse ran to Little Ant and
lifted up the leaf.

'Thank you, Cousin Flea!' called Little Ant.

Little Ant ran back to her nice,
warm home under the ground.
'I'm back, Mum!' Little Ant called.
'Hello, Little Ant,' said her mother.
'I am glad you're home!'

2 📝 Story map

A story map shows what happens in a story.

A story often begins with a **problem** and ends with a **solution**.

Complete the story map for *Little Ant*.

Problem: A ___ falls on Little Ant.

What happens:

1   She says to the leaf, 'Please get off me'.
2   She says to the mouse, 'Please lift up the leaf'.
3   She says to the cat, 'Please chase ___ '.
4   ___
5   ___

Solution:

1   The flea ___
2   ___
3   ___
4   ___

3 💬 Verbs in the story

Find these words in the story.

blow   shiver   lift up   chase   scare   bite

Talk about their meaning with your class.

Take turns acting out one of the words for your partner to guess.

Then find the past simple form of each verb in the story.

4 💬 Puppet play

Make puppets for the characters in the story (including the leaf!).

Act out the story.

6 Choose a project — How are bugs special?

A Write bug riddles

- Write riddles about bugs.
- Draw pictures or find photos.
- Your classmates must match the riddles with the pictures.

Who am I? I have 4 short legs and 2 long legs.

Who am I? I make silk.

a cricket

a silkworm

B Perform a poem

- Read and learn a poem.
- Draw pictures. Then perform it.

Fuzzy wuzzy caterpillar
Into a corner will creep.
She'll spin herself a blanket
And then go fast asleep.
Fuzzy wuzzy caterpillar
Will wake up by and by,
To find that she has grown two wings.
Now she's a butterfly!

C Create a cartoon story

- Draw and write a cartoon story comparing a boy and a bug.
- First choose a bug.
- Write what the boy says.
- Then draw your cartoon bug and write what your bug says.

I have 2 eyes.

I have 8 eyes.

LOOk what I can do!

- I can name and describe bugs.

- I can say how spiders and insects are similar and different.

- I can read and write words with the long **e** sound.

- I can write questions and answer them.

- I can read, discuss and act out a story.

89

7 Our green Earth

1 Think about it   How can we care for the Earth?

61 1 Read and listen

Act out the words.

The sky is painted blue

I'm glad the sky is painted blue
And the Earth is painted green,
With such a lot of nice fresh air
All sandwiched in between.

62 2 Rules in the park

Dad and Su Lyn are talking to the park keeper.

What can you do in the park? What mustn't you do?

Unit 7 Lesson 1 **Vocabulary:** in the park **Use of English:** impersonal *you; must/mustn't* with rules; *no* + *-ing* form; *can* for permission
Read/Listen: *The sky is painted blue*; aural comprehension **Write:** a poem

Listen, point and say. Answer the questions you hear.

sign   rules   grass

cycling   fishing   sandwich   bin   litter

4 Follow the rules!

Look at each picture. What mustn't you do?

a   b   c   d

Now find the matching sign in the big picture.

5 Write a poem

- Read out the poem to your partner. It's a *haiku*, a special kind of poem. Poets in Japan wrote the first *haikus* a long time ago.

- Write a new poem about nature.

An old silent pond ...
A frog jumps into the pond,
Splash! Silence again.

Matsuo Basho

2 Find out more — Why are trees important?

64 **1** 🔬 **Before you read**

What do you know about trees? Say five facts. Then listen and read to learn more facts.

Presents from a tree

① The green **leaves** reach high into the air. They clean the dirty air. They give us fresh air to breathe.

② Some trees give us **fruit**, like lemons and cherries. Other trees give us nuts.

③ People use the **wood** to make fires for cooking and for warmth. They build houses and boats and furniture. They use wood to make paper.

④ The **roots** reach down into the ground. They hold the soil in place for other plants and grass.

Disappearing trees

All over the world, people are cutting down trees. People cut down trees to make room for new buildings. They cut down trees to get more wood and make more paper.

When trees are cut down, animals lose their homes. There are fewer trees to clean the air and hold the soil in place.

Unit 7 Lesson 2 Use of English: *will* for future intentions/promises; *What does ... mean?* **Listen/Read:** for information **Talk:** discussing and applying information **Write:** guided writing

Help save the trees!

Children all over the world can help to save trees.
In some schools, children plant trees.
In many schools, children recycle paper.
A factory uses the old paper to make
new paper. So fewer trees are cut down.

2 Talk about it

What new facts did you learn about trees?
Think of some foods that come from trees.
Look around your room.

Name things that are made from wood.
(Don't forget that paper is made from wood!)

3 What does it mean?

Are there any words in the text that you
don't know?

Ask your class:

If nobody knows,
look it up!

> What does **factory** mean?

4 What will you do to save trees?

Here are some ways to save trees:

> What will you do
> to save trees?

Plant a tree.

Recycle paper.

Write on both sides of your paper.

Dry your hands with only one paper towel.

Use your pictures to wrap presents.

> I will recycle
> paper.

What will you do? Have a conversation. Make a promise.

3 Words and sounds   Long o

1 Missing words

Look at the picture. Fill in the missing word. Say the sentence.

1 In the ground there is a ___ .   **4** On the branch there is a ___ .

2 In the hole there is a ___ .   **5** In the nest there is a ___ .

3 On the tree there is a ___ .   **6** On the bird there are some ___ .

65 2 🎵 **Listen and sing**

The green grass grew all around

There was a **hole** in the middle of the **ground**,
The prettiest hole that you ever did see.
Well, the **hole** in the **ground**,

Chorus And the green grass grew all around and around,
The green grass grew all around.

And in that **hole** there was a **tree**,
The prettiest tree that you ever did see.
Well, the **tree** in the **hole**,
And the **hole** in the **ground**,

Chorus

And on that **tree** there was a **branch** ...
And on that **branch** there was a **nest** ...
And in that **nest** there was a **bird** ...
And on that **bird** there were some **feathers** ...

feathers
bird
tree
branch
nest
hole

3 📝 💬 [AB] Long o spellings o and ow

Which word has the long o sound: **hole** or **ground**?

Write these words:

grow no slowly boat road rope goes home goat toes.

Underline the letters that make the long o sound.

With a partner, write two sentences. Each sentence must have
two or more words with a long o sound.

66 4 The sounds of ow

The letters **ow** can make the long o sound in **slow**.
The letters **ow** can also make the sound in **cow**.

That **cow** is
very **slow**!

Read and listen to the poem.
In which words do the letters **ow** rhyme with **slow**?
In which words do they rhyme with **cow**?

Five little seeds

Under the leaves,
And under the snow,
Five little seeds are
Waiting to grow.
Out comes the sun,
Down comes a shower.
And up come five
Pretty pink flowers.

Language detective

Some words from the song have an
ow sound in the middle, like in **cow**.

ground   around

Which letters make that sound?

4 Use of English   At the market

67 **1 Choosing a plant**

A little boy and his dad are choosing
a plant at the market. Listen.
Which vegetable does the boy like?
Which one do you like?

2 💬 **What is this? What are these?**

Pretend you are the little boy in the
picture opposite. Point to the plants.
Ask questions. Your partner will answer.

onions

peppers

tomatoes

beans

carrots

potatoes

> What is **this?**

> **This** is
> a bean plant.

> What are **these?**

> **These** are
> carrot plants.

Language tip

We use **this** for **one** thing.
We use **these** for **two or
more** things.

3 💬 AB **What must you do?**

Tell the little boy how to look after the
bean plant. Can you put the pictures in
the right order?

a Water the
plant.

b Dig a hole.

c Fill the hole
with soil.

d Put the plant
in the hole.

Say the four instructions to your partner.

Close the book. Can you remember what to do?

> You must dig a hole.
> Then ...

96

4 Would you like some?

Listen to the woman buying some fruit. What fruit does she buy?

Now read the conversation. Listen again.

Can you fill in the missing words from the *Word box*?

Woman: What __ fruit!

Fruit seller: Thank you. Would you like __?

Woman: Yes, I'd like two __ , please.

Fruit seller: Are __ OK?

Woman: Yes, those look great.

Fruit seller: Anything else?

Woman: Yes. A pineapple, __ .

Fruit seller: How about __ one?

Woman: Yes, that one looks nice. Thank you.

Fruit seller: You're welcome.

Word box

mangoes	nice
please	this
these	some

Language tip

We use **this** and **these** for things that are very near us. We use **that** and **those** for things that are less near.

5 🗨 Act it out

Take turns being the buyer and the seller.

Practise the conversation. Ask for your favourite fruits!

I'd like a pear, please.

Is this one OK?

69 **1** AB **Before you read**

You are going to read a **biography** – the true story of someone's life. This is the biography of Wangari Maathai. She lived in Kenya, in Africa. She worked to save the trees in Kenya. How do you think she did this?

Wangari Maathai: 'Mama Trees'

Wangari Maathai was born in 1940 in a small village in Kenya. Green trees covered the land. Families grew food in small gardens. A little river brought clean water to the village. Women and children picked figs and other fruit from the trees. They used wood to make fires for cooking. Wangari loved her green and beautiful home.

When Wangari grew older, she went away to school. She studied in the United States and in Germany.

When Wangari came back to Kenya, the land
was very different. The family gardens had gone.
The trees had gone. The sun had dried the earth.
The wind had blown away the soil.
The little river was dry.

The people in Wangari's village now worked for a
big company. They grew tea that was sold to people
in other countries. Women and children walked a
long way to get clean water and firewood.

Wangari felt very sad. What could she do to help?
An idea came to her. She would plant trees. Kenya
could become green and beautiful again.

Wangari took seeds from trees.
She planted the seeds in her garden.
She watched them and watered them.
The seeds grew into little trees.

Wangari gave the little trees to the women and children in her village. Together they planted rows and rows of little trees. Every day, the women and children watered the trees. The trees grew. Soon there were figs and other fruits to eat. There was clean water in the little rivers.

There was wood for fires to cook food.

'When we plant trees, we plant the seeds of peace and hope,' said Wangari.

People all over Africa planted trees. They wanted to do the same as Wangari.

Millions of trees were planted. People named Wangari 'Mama Trees'. She became very famous.

'Little things make a big difference,' said Wangari. 'My little thing is planting trees.'

2 True or false?

Read each sentence. Is it **true** or **false**?

1 When Wangari was a child, there were no trees.

2 Wangari was sad because the trees had gone.

3 Many people planted little trees in long rows.

4 People cut down all the new trees.

5 The new trees made Kenya a better place to live.

3 What happened first? What happened next?

Work with your partner to put these sentences in order.

___ Wangari planted the seeds and watered them.

_1_ Wangari took seeds from the trees.

___ The trees grew big. Fruit grew on the trees.

___ Wangari gave the little trees to women and children in her village.

___ Together they planted many rows of trees.

> **Words to remember**
>
> Find these words in the story:
> grew   were   gone   little.
> Practise spelling them.

4 Write your autobiography

A biography is the true story of someone's life.
An autobiography is the story of your own life.
In your autobiography, write:

- where you were born
- two interesting things that have happened to you
- how old you were when each thing happened
- what you would like to do when you grow up.

I was born in Seoul.

6 Choose a project   How can we care for the Earth?

A Make a poster: Be kind to our planet

- Think of some nice things you can do for the Earth.

> You can pick up litter.
> You can recycle bottles or paper.

- What else can you do?
- Make a poster for each idea.

Be kind to our planet!
Plant a tree!

B Make a book about your heroes

Wangari Maathai is a hero to many people.
She made the world a better place.

- Think of someone you know who makes the world a better place. Perhaps they help people or animals? Perhaps they keep your town or school safe? Perhaps they make beautiful things?

- Make a book with your friends. Write about a different hero on each page.

- Each person must write a page about their hero.

> My grandma is my hero. She cares for all the children.

C Learn a poem

Read, learn and act out the poem.

- Draw pictures of a garden growing.

What makes a garden grow, grow, grow?
Lots of work with a rake and hoe,
Little seeds planted in a row –
That makes a garden grow, grow, grow.

What brings the little plants up from the ground?
Rain from the sky coming down, down,
Bright yellow sunlight all around,
Help bring the little plants up from the ground.

LOOk what I can do!

- I can talk about rules.

- I can talk about trees and why they are important.

- I can read words with the long **o** sound and the spelling **ow**.

- I can go shopping for plants and fruit.

- I can read and discuss a biography.

8 Home, sweet home

1 Think about it
What kinds of homes do people and animals build?

70 1 Read and listen

Find the animal homes in the picture.

Homes

A nest is a home for a bird.

A hive is a home for a bee.

A hole is a home for a rabbit.

And a house is a home for me.

71 2 A tree house

Listen to Mia talk about the tree house near her home.

How do you get to the second floor? Can all children go there?

Unit 8 Lesson 1 Vocabulary: home **Use of English:** present perfect: *Have you ever …?*; have + object + infinitive **Listen:** *Homes*; aural comprehension **Talk:** What's in the basket?

Listen, point and say. Answer the questions.

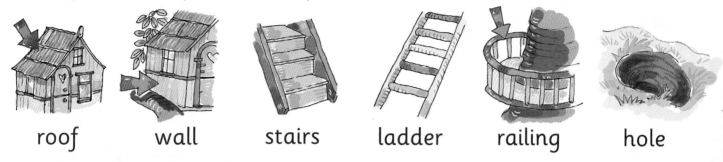

roof   wall   stairs   ladder   railing   hole

4 💬 Talk about it

Read the questions. Talk to your partner. Then tell the class.

1 Have you ever been in a tree house?

2 Did the tree house have a ladder or stairs?

3 Have you ever seen a beehive? Where was it?

4 Have you ever seen a rabbit? What colour was it?

5 Name some animals that live in a tree.

6 Name some animals that live in a hole in the ground.

5 💬 What's in the basket?

What have Mia and Jenna got in their basket? Fill in the missing words.

> They've got some __ to read, some __ to eat and some __ to drink.

What would you put in your basket to read, to eat and to drink?

bananas   books   juice   crisps   magazines   water

73 1 Before you read

People build different houses in different parts of the world.
Do you have houses like these in your country?

Different kinds of homes

Beehive houses

In some hot, dry places, people build houses from mud. They mix mud with water and dry grass. These houses are called beehive houses. The thick mud walls keep the homes cool.

1 Beehive houses in Syria

Stilt houses

In some hot, wet places, people build houses on stilts. Stilt houses are built high above the water or land. The 'stilts' are tree trunks. The air blows under the houses and keeps them cool.

2 Stilt houses in Borneo

Cave houses

Cave homes are built in rocks and mountains. Some cave homes are very old. Cave homes stay cool during the summer. They stay warm during the winter.

3 Cave houses in Turkey

Skyscrapers

In cities all over the world, people live in tall buildings called skyscrapers. Skyscrapers are made of metal, concrete and glass. This skyscraper has more than 160 floors and 57 lifts!

4 Burj Khalifa skyscraper in Dubai

2 True or false?

Look at the text. Is each statement **true** or **false**?

1 A beehive house has lots of windows.

2 A skyscraper has lots of windows.

3 A cave home keeps you warm in winter.

4 Stilt houses are built only in cold, dry places.

3 Where do they live?

Read the clues. Which home does each child live in?

To get to my home, I go up in a lift.

To get to my home, I ride in a boat.

My home has one room. The room is round, like a circle.

My bedroom is inside a mountain!

a

Layla

b

Mohammed

c

Ahmed

d

Harika

74 **1** **Let's build a cool house!**

Listen and read these instructions. Look at the words in **red**.
What sound do you hear in these words?

You can build a **cool** house with boxes.
You will need sticky tape, **glue** and scissors.
Use some **tubes**, **too**.
Will **you** build a castle or a stilt house?
Will your house have one **room**
or a **few** rooms?

Find words above that rhyme with **zoo**. The vowel
sound has different spellings. Find words where
the vowel has the same spelling as:

zoo blue new.

75 **2** **The sounds of oo**

The letters **oo** often stand for the vowel sound in **too** and **zoo**.
Listen to these words:

goose moon roof food.

Then use them to talk about the picture.

Sometimes the letters **oo** stand for
a different sound.
Listen and say these words:

wood foot book look.

Use these words to talk about the picture.

3 💬 **What will you put in your house?**

This house is made of cardboard boxes. It has got four rooms.

Look at the pictures. Listen to the children talking about where to put the things. Where will they put the bed, the sink and the TV?
Now talk to your partner. Where will you put the things?

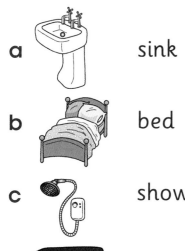

a sink

b bed

c shower

d TV

e toilet

f table

g cooker

h chair

i cupboard

j bookcase

> How about putting the TV in the living room?

> That's a good idea.

> Let's put the bed in the bedroom.

> OK!

4 📝 **Make and write**

Make a little house or some things to put in a house.
You can use paper or cardboard, scissors and sticky tape.
Or you can use other things. Write some sentences about it.

4 Use of English Making choices

(77) 1 What would you like in your playground?

These children are going to have a new playground!
The playground designer is asking them what they
would like in their playground. Listen and point to the
things that the children choose.

tunnel   bridge

2 💬 Design your own playground!

What would *you* choose for your playground?
Ask and answer questions with your partner.

3 📝 Draw and write

Draw a picture of your playground.
Write a description.

> My playground will have __ and __ .
> It will have __ too.

Language tip

We can use **too** when we add something more.
I'd like a bridge and I'd like a swing **too**.

What would you like
in your playground?

I'd like two ladders, please.

OK, would you like
rope ladders or
wooden ladders?

Unit 8 Lesson 4 Use of English: past simple questions and answers; *Would you like …or …? / I'd like* **Vocabulary:** *too* to add information; *will* for future intention
Listen/Talk: aural comprehension **Write:** guided writing **Song:** *The princess in the tower* **Talk:** asking and answering questions

4 🎵 **Listen and sing**

This song tells a story. Listen and join in.
Are there words in the song that you don't
know? Ask what the words mean.

The princess in the tower

There was a princess long ago,
Long ago, long ago.
There was a princess long ago,
Long, long ago.

And she lived in a big high tower ...
A naughty fairy waved her wand ...
The princess slept for a hundred years ...
A great big forest grew around ...
A handsome prince came riding by ...
He took his sword and chopped it down ...
He kissed her hand to wake her up ...
So everybody's happy now!

> What does **princess** mean?

fairy

princess

tower

wand

forest

sword   prince

5 💬 **Ask and answer questions**

1 Where **did** the princess **live**?

2 Why **did** the princess **fall** asleep?

3 How long **did** the princess **sleep**?

4 How **did** the prince **get** through the forest?

5 How **did** the prince **wake** the princess up?

> The princess **lived** ____
> She **fell** asleep
> because ____

6 📝 **Tell the story with pictures**

Draw pictures to show what happened. Write sentences below the pictures.

1 💬 **Before you read**

Work in groups of three. Each person in the group reads one of the texts: *Rabbit homes, Beaver homes* or *Termite homes.* Then share what you have learned with children who read the other texts.

Where do animals build homes?

Rabbit homes

Most rabbits build their home under
the ground. A rabbit home has lots of tunnels.
Some tunnels lead to rooms where the rabbits sleep.
There are special rooms for baby rabbits and their mother.

Every rabbit home has lots of rabbit holes.
The rabbits use these holes to go in and out.
When a rabbit sees a fox or other enemy,
it stamps on the ground with its back foot.
The other rabbits hear the sound.
They run down a rabbit hole.

A rabbit home keeps rabbits
warm, dry and safe from enemies.

rabbit hole

room for baby rabbits

tunnel

Beaver homes

Beavers build homes from branches, rocks and mud.
They build their home in the middle of a pond.

The beavers cut down trees with their sharp teeth.
They make a huge pile of branches.

The beavers build a living room in the
middle of their home.
The floor of the room is above the water.
The beavers and their babies live in this room.
It is warm and dry.

Beavers enter their home through underwater doors.
This keeps their home safe from wolves and other enemies.

The beavers' home keeps beavers safe,
dry and warm all year long.

branches, rock and mud

underwater door

Termite homes

The tallest animal home is built by tiny insects called termites. The termites use mud to build their homes.

Some termites build huge towers.
They live in the towers and in the ground below.

The termites' home has lots of tunnels and rooms.
In the middle of the home, there is a room for the queen.
The queen lays eggs.

Some termites build rooms that are gardens.
They grow a special mushroom in these gardens.
The termites eat these mushrooms.

The termites build air holes to keep their home cool when the weather is hot.

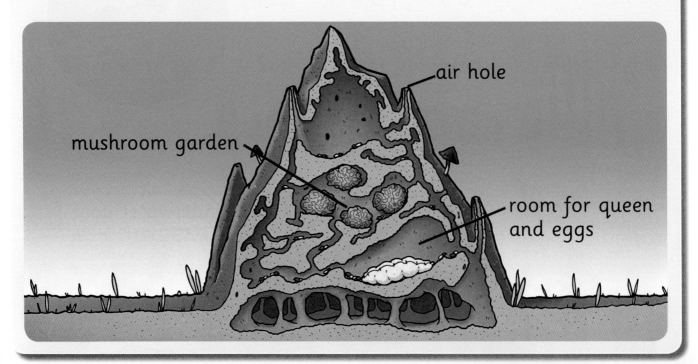

mushroom garden

air hole

room for queen and eggs

2 💬 New words

Find two words in the text that you didn't know.
Find out what the words mean. Teach the words
to your group.

3 💬 Share your information

Meet in your group of three. Answer these questions
about **rabbits**, **beavers** and **termites**.

1 Where does your animal build its home?

2 What is the home made of?

3 Does it have rooms?

4 Who lives in the rooms?

5 Why is it a good home?

4 💬 Which animal home?

Answer these questions with your group.

1 Which animal home has a garden inside?

2 Which animal home is made of wood?

3 Which animal home has doors under the water?

4 Which animal stamps its foot when it sees an enemy?

5 Which animal home looks like a beehive house?

6 Which animal's enemy is a fox?

Language detective

Cool means quite cold, but not too
cold. Find a word in the texts which
means quite hot but not too hot.

w_ _ _

Words to remember

Find these words in the story:

their   down   middle   with.

Practise spelling them.

6 Choose a project — What kinds of homes do people and animals build?

A Write about an animal home

- Choose an animal.

- Look up information about that animal's home in a book or on the Internet.

  Where does the animal build its home?

  What is the home made of?

- Find some interesting facts about the home.

- Draw a picture.

ant	spider	turtle	owl	mouse	monkey

B Design a play room for children

- What will you put in the play room?

  - A huge TV?

  - A ping-pong table?

  - Ropes and slides?

  - What else?

- Make a poster.

- Draw a picture of the room.

- Write words on the picture.

c Write a poem

- Write two new verses for the poem *Homes* on page 104.
- Draw pictures. You can write about homes for animals or homes for things! For example:

> A sock is a home for a foot.
> A bin is a home for litter.

You can use the sentence starters below or think of other ideas.

> A shell is a home for a ___ .
> A box is a home for a ___ .

LOOk what I can do!

- I can talk about parts of a house.

- I can talk about different kinds of homes.

- I can read words with the long **u** sound.

- I can ask about and make choices: **Would you like __ or __ ?**

- I can read and talk about an information text.

1 Think about it — What can we do in the town and the countryside?

80 1 Read and listen

Do you live in a city? Have you ever seen a rainbow?

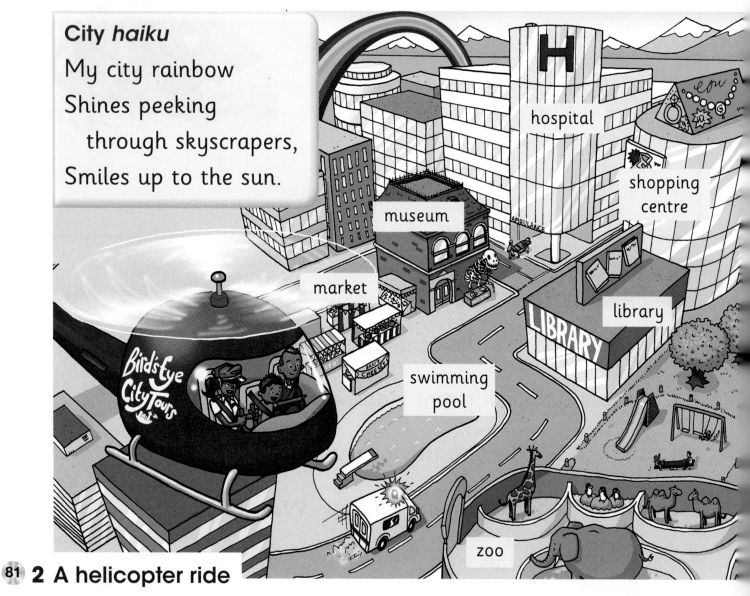

City *haiku*

My city rainbow
Shines peeking
    through skyscrapers,
Smiles up to the sun.

hospital

shopping centre

museum

market

library

swimming pool

zoo

81 2 A helicopter ride

Malik and his dad are going for a ride in a helicopter.
What must they do before they start? Point to the things that they see.

3 Topic vocabulary

Listen, point and say. Answer the questions.

helicopter

safety belt

hospital

ambulance

shopping centre

---

81 **4** 💬 **Who says it?**

Read and decide who says it: Malik, Dad or the pilot.
Listen again and check.

1 Would you like to sit by the window?

2 We must wear our safety belts.

3 Wow! I can see everything!

4 I don't like shopping.

5 I love this helicopter ride!

83 **5** 💬 **So do I!**

Listen to the conversation.
Do Dad and Malik like the same things?

	Dad	Malik
Going to the library	☺	☺
Helicopters	☺	☺
Shopping	☺	☹

Say some things that you like.
Does your partner like the same things?

I like football.

So do I!

I like spiders.

I don't!

84 **1 Before you read**

Have you ever been to an inside or outside café?
Read and choose which café you would like to go to.

Cafés
The Jungle Café

This café is in a town. The café is inside
a building, but it looks like a jungle!
You can hear jungle birds and insects.
You can see some jungle animals and
some fish. There is a menu for adults
and a menu for children.
The food is delicious!

The Tree House Café

This café is in the countryside. The café
is outside. In fact, it's in a tree house!
To get to the café, you walk up some
stairs, then you climb up a ladder.
You can hold the railing while you
climb. You can hear a musician playing
the guitar. You can sit and look up at
the trees or down at the ground.
The café is open in summer and closed
in winter.

2 Which café?

Say which café each sentence is about: the Jungle Café, the Tree House Café, or both cafés?

1 It is inside a building.

2 It is closed in winter.

3 You can hear music there.

4 You must climb up a ladder to get there.

5 You can see leaves and branches.

6 You can watch the fish.

85 3 What would you like to eat and drink?

Look at the menu. Listen to Josh and Rosa talking to the waiter. What food and drinks do they order?

4 Over to you!

Work with a partner. One of you is the waiter and one is the customer. Order some food from the menu.

Waiter

Would you like something to drink?

How about some lemonade?

Customer

I'd like some apple juice, please.

Can I have some honey cake?

86 1 🎵 **Sing an opposites song**

Listen and join in. Half of the class sing the **blue** words. Half the class sing the **green** words. All the class sing the **black** words.

Opposites

When I say day,
I say night.
When I say black,
I say white.
When I go left,
I go right.
We're opposites!
When I say yes,
I say no.
When I say 'Stop!'
I say 'Go!'
When I sing high,
I sing low.

Chorus

We're opposites.
You and me, we're different
as can be,
We always disagree –
opposites.

I sit,
I stand.

But we go hand in hand,
On water or on land,
Opposites.

When I'm lost,
I am found.
When I'm up,
I am down.
When I smile,
I will frown,
We're opposites!
When I'm weak,
I am strong.
When I'm right,
I am wrong.
When I PING,
I will PONG.

Chorus

Curt Bright

2 💬 AB How many syllables?

Clap the syllables for these city words. How many syllables are there? If there are two or more syllables, clap loudly on the strong syllable and clap quietly on the weaker syllables.

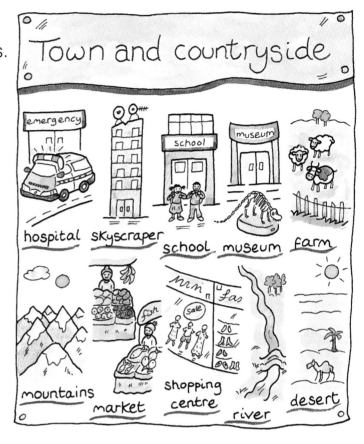

Town and countryside

hospital skyscraper school museum farm

mountains market shopping centre river desert

87 3 📝 💬 Write a desert *haiku*

Read this *haiku*. The desert is a hot, dry place where it doesn't rain much. Is there a desert near you?

The desert is nice.

The sun shines on the desert.

I like the desert.

Count the number of syllables in each line. Now write a *haiku* about your favourite place.

- Line 1 will have 5 syllables.
- Line 2 will have 7 syllables.
- Line 3 will have 5 syllables.

Our playground is ____

4 Use of English   Choosing and comparing

88 **1 Choosing a holiday**

Josh and Rosa's family want to go on holiday. Listen. Where would Josh and Rosa like to go? What would they like to do there?

mountains

beach

amusement park

Word box

swim	play
climb	have fun
go to	see

city

desert

2 Where would you like to go?

Look at the photos on this page. Ask and answer questions with your partner. You can use words from the *Word box*.

> Where would you like to go?

> I'd like to go to an amusement park.

> What would you like to do there?

> I'd like to play on the slide.

3 Draw and write

Draw a picture of a place where you would like to go. Write a sentence.

4 Comparing places

Do you agree with Rosa or Josh?

> The beach is **nicer than** the mountains.

> The mountains are **more exciting than** the beach.

Language detective

When we compare things:

We often add **-r** or **-er** for words with one syllable: **nicer than, colder than**

We often use **more** for words with two syllables or more: **more exciting than**

Talk about the places in the photos on page 124. Use the words in the *Word box*:

> The desert is hotter than the mountains.

> The city is more exciting than the desert.

Word box

hotter than
colder than
nicer than

more exciting than
more fun than
more scary than
more beautiful than

Language detective

Look at this:

The beach is good. The amusement park is fun.

But ... the beach is **better than** the amusement park.

DON'T SAY The beach is ~~gooder~~ than the amusement park.

That's wrong!

> I'm **better than** all the other birds!

> No, you're not!

5 Read and respond

1 Before you read

Some people like the city. Some people like the countryside.
How about you? As you read this story, ask yourself,
'Am I a **city mouse** or a **country mouse**?'

The city mouse and the country mouse

Cindy, the city mouse, and Callie, the country mouse,
met on the TV show, *Changing Places*.

'Welcome to *Changing Places*!' said the announcer.
'On this show, you change places for a week.'

'I've never been to the city,' said Callie.
'I've never been to the country,' said Cindy.
'Let's change places!' said Callie and Cindy.

'You'll love the city,' said Cindy.
'There is so much to see and do.
There is always something happening.'

'Wow,' said Callie. 'That sounds great.
The country is wonderful too.
The bees buzz and the birds sing.
At night you can count the stars.'

'That sounds wonderful,' said Cindy.

That evening, Callie arrived in the city.
The city streets were full of life.
There were shops and cafés, bright
lights and music.

Some mice waved to Callie.
'Hi Callie, welcome to the city,'
they said. 'We're Cindy's friends.
Come to our party.'

The party was at the top of a
high building. There was food
and dancing. 'This is amazing,'
said Callie. 'I love the city.'
'So do we!' said Cindy's friends.

Just then there was a strange noise.
'What's that?' asked Callie.
'It's a cat,' shouted the other mice.
'Run for your life!'

Callie ran out of the door, down
the stairs, and into the street.
She jumped into a taxi.
'Take me home,' she said.
'The city is too scary for me.
I want to go back to the country.'

That same evening, Cindy arrived in the country. Callie's friend, Carlos, met Cindy at the bus stop. 'Welcome to the country, Cindy,' he said. 'My name is Carlos.'

'Would you like to have a picnic?' Carlos and Cindy ate fresh berries and nuts. They listened to the birds sing. The sky grew dark and the stars came out.

'This is beautiful,' said Cindy. 'I love the country.' 'So do I!' said Carlos.

Just then Carlos shouted, 'Quickly! Run and hide. Here comes an owl!'

Cindy and Carlos jumped down a mouse hole just in time. The owl flew away.

Cindy hurried to the bus stop. 'Thank you for the picnic, Carlos,' she said. 'But the country is too scary for me. I'm going back to the city.'

That night, in the country, Callie said, 'I'm so happy to be home!'

That night, in the city, Cindy said, 'I'm so happy to be home!'

2 💬 **Talk about it**

1 What did Callie like about the city?

2 What didn't Callie like about the city?

3 What did Cindy like about the country?

4 What didn't Cindy like about the country?

3 💬 **Act out the story**

Which character will you be?

4 📝 **Write and draw**

Which do you like better, the city or the country? What do you like about it? Draw a picture of you in the city or the country. Write some sentences.

Words to remember

Find these words in the story:

something   want   great   come.

Practise spelling them.

Language detective

Can you remember another word which means the same as **city**?

What can we do in the town and the countryside?

A Make a book of poems

- Write poems, perhaps *haikus*, about your favourite places.

- Draw a picture for each poem.

- Make a cover for your book.

- Write the title and authors' names on the cover.

Poems about
our
favourite places

By Malik, Josh and Sam

B Make your own café

- Where would you like to have your café?

- Choose a name for your café.

- Make a menu.

- Act out a conversation at your café: you can be a waiter and customers.

Would you like something to drink?

Menu

c Make a travel poster

- The title of the poster is:
  Where would you like to go?

- Draw pictures, or find photos, of places you would like to go to for a holiday.

- Write why they are nice places for a holiday. Write what you can do there.

Where would you like to go?

LOOk what I can do!

- I can talk about places I like.

- I can say what I would like to eat and drink.

- I can count syllables.

- I can compare places.

- I can read, talk about and act out a story.

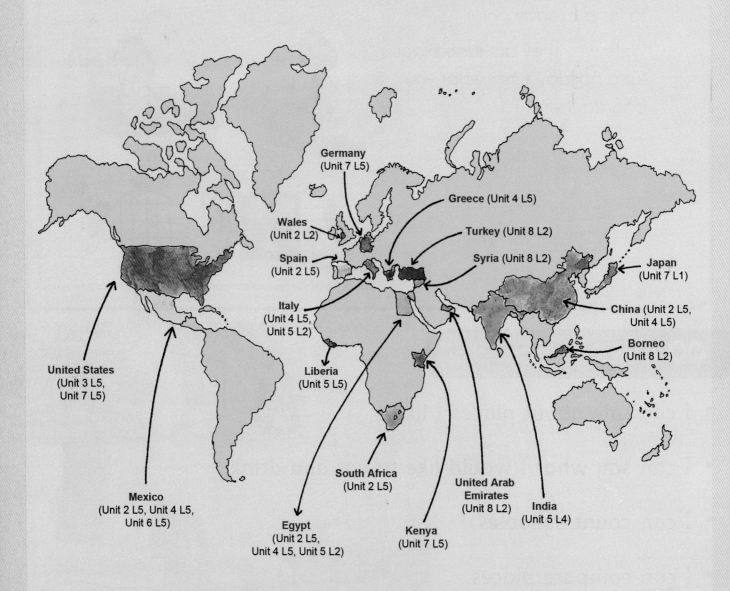

Germany
(Unit 7 L5)

Greece (Unit 4 L5)

Wales
(Unit 2 L2)

Turkey (Unit 8 L2)

Spain
(Unit 2 L5)

Syria (Unit 8 L2)

Japan
(Unit 7 L1)

Italy
(Unit 4 L5,
Unit 5 L2)

China (Unit 2 L5,
Unit 4 L5)

Borneo
(Unit 8 L2)

United States
(Unit 3 L5,
Unit 7 L5)

Liberia
(Unit 5 L5)

Mexico
(Unit 2 L5, Unit 4 L5,
Unit 6 L5)

South Africa
(Unit 2 L5)

United Arab
Emirates
(Unit 8 L2)

India
(Unit 5 L4)

Egypt
(Unit 2 L5,
Unit 4 L5, Unit 5 L2)

Kenya
(Unit 7 L5)

2 Months of the year

January 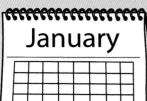	February 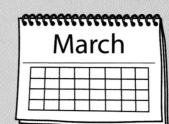	March 	April 
May 	June 	July 	August 
September 	October 	November	December

3 Days of the week

Monday   Tuesday   Wednesday   Thursday

Friday   Saturday   Sunday

4 Times of day

morning   afternoon   evening   night

5 Numbers 1–20

1 – one	6 – six	11 – eleven	16 – sixteen
2 – two	7 – seven	12 – twelve	17 – seventeen
3 – three	8 – eight	13 – thirteen	18 – eighteen
4 – four	9 – nine	14 – fourteen	19 – nineteen
5 – five	10 – ten	15 – fifteen	20 – twenty

6 Numbers 21–100

21 – twenty-one	30 – thirty	70 – seventy
22 – twenty-two	40 – forty	80 – eighty
23 – twenty-three	50 – fifty	90 – ninety
24 – twenty-four	60 – sixty	100 – one hundred

7 What time is it?

morning   1:00

afternoon   04:00

8 Colours

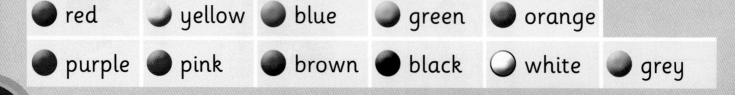

● red   ● yellow   ● blue   ● green   ● orange

● purple   ● pink   ● brown   ● black   ○ white   ● grey

9 The body and clothes

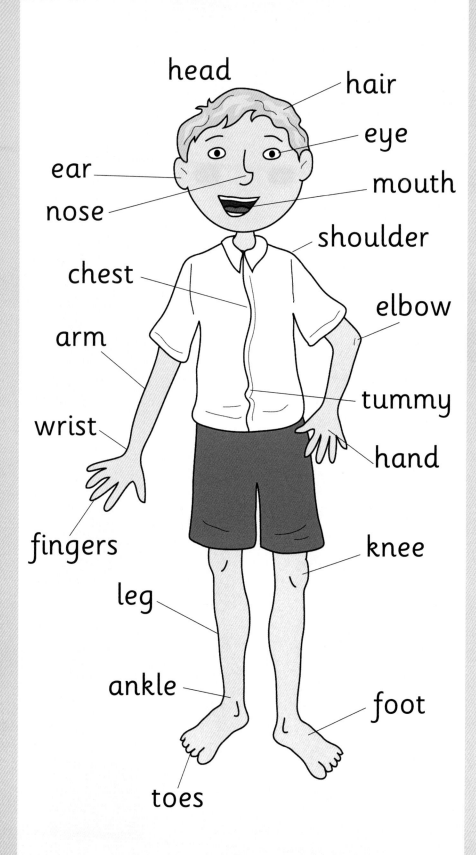

head
hair
eye
ear
nose
mouth
shoulder
chest
elbow
arm
tummy
wrist
hand
fingers
knee
leg
ankle
foot
toes

shoes
sock
hat
skirt
shirt
dress
boots
glasses
jacket
jumper
backpack
trousers

Bedroom

Bathroom

Living room

Kitchen

This house has got four rooms.

bed

chair

cooker

cupboard

shower

sink

table

toilet

TV

book

bookcase

boy

children

clock

computer

crayons

cupboard

dictionary

girl

glue

map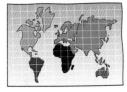

paintbrush

paper

paper clip

pen

pencil

playground

ruler

scissors

slide

swing

tablet

teacher

12 Food

apple

banana

bread

cake

carrot

cheese

cherries

egg

grape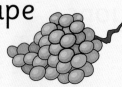

juice

lemonade

mango

milk

nuts

onion

orange

pear

pineapple

pizza

potato

rice

sandwich

soup

tomato

ambulance

apartment building

bicycle

boat

bridge

bus

café

car

factory

helicopter

hospital

library

market

museum

park

people

plane

shop

shopping centre

skyscraper

street

swimming pool

train

zoo

actor

architect

artist

astronomer

baker

clothes designer

computer programmer

dancer

doctor

farmer

firefighter

football player

musician

nurse

painter

pilot

police officer

scientist

singer

street cleaner

taxi driver

teacher

writer

zookeeper

15 Animals

ant

bear

bee

bird

butterfly

cat

cow

deer

dog

duck

elephant

fish

fox

frog

goat

goose

hen

horse

mouse

rabbit

shark

spider

turtle

whale

16 Actions

build (built) 	catch (caught) 	climb 
cut (cut) 	draw (drew) 	eat (ate) 
fall (fell) 	fly (flew) 	jump 
measure 	play 	read (read) 
run (ran) 	sit (sat) 	stand (stood) 
swim (swam) 	talk 	throw (threw) 
walk 	wave 	write (wrote) 

beach

cloud

day

desert

farm

flower

grass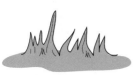

jungle

leaf

moon

mountain

night

pond

rain

rainbow

river

rock

shadow

shell

snow

stars

sun

tree

wind

Acknowledgements

The authors and publishers would like to thank the following for their contribution to the development of Stage 2.
Series Editor: Kathryn Harper; Development Editor: Frances Reynolds; Reviewers: Nahla El Geyoushi; Lois Hopkins, MA Publishing; Ana Pérez Moreno, Licentiate in English Language and in Education; Claire Olmez, BEd MA ELT; Mary Spratt.

Cover artwork: Bill Bolton

The authors and publishers acknowledge the following sources of copyright material and are grateful for the permissions granted. While every effort has been made, it has not always been possible to identify the sources of all the material used, or to trace all copyright holders. If any omissions are brought to our notice, we will be happy to include the appropriate acknowledgements on reprinting.

Text
p. 6 "Reading" from RHYMES ABOUT US by Marchette Chute, published 1974 by E.P. Dutton. Used by permission of Elizabeth Hauser.
p. 28 "A Lot of Kids" from THE BUTTERFLY JAR by Jeff Moss, copyright ©1989 by Jeff Moss. Reprinted by permission of International Creative Management, Inc. Used by permission of Bantam Books, a division of Random House, Inc. Any third party use of this material outside of this publication is prohibited. Interested parties must apply directly to Random House, Inc. for permission.
p. 122 "Opposites" written and used by permission of Curt Bright of The String Beans.

Other songs and music throughout are reproduced from Primary Music Box © Cambridge University Press.

Photographs
p8 a celeste clochard / fotolia , b Rikke / Shutterstock, c Angelo Giampiccolo / Shutterstock, d Doug Houghton / Alamy; p9 tl Sandra van der Steen / Thinkstock, tr mkkuppuraj / Thinkstock, bl Rahha / Shutterstock, br Rohit Seth / Shutterstock; p25 t Lammeyer / iStockphoto, c l-r way out west photography / Alamy, imagebroker / Alamy, marilyn barbone / Shutterstock, Robert Hardholt / Thinkstock, b Marcus Lindström / iStockphoto; p30 a Monkey Business / Thinkstock, b Don Bayley / iStock / Thinkstock, c auremar / Shutterstock, d Galushko Sergey / Shutterstock, e Tracy Whiteside / iStock / Thinkstock; p36 t Dstamatelos / iStockphoto, c Stefan Christmann / Corbis, b Jaap2 / iStockphoto; p39 t l-r Ingram Publishing / Thinkstock; Csaba Peterdi / Shutterstock, skynesher / iStockphoto, Pete Pahham / Shutterstock, pkujiahe/ iStockphoto, emre ogan / iStockphoto, b l-r ktaylorg / iStockphoto; Jasmin Merdan / fotolia; p41 a Edwin Verin / iStock / Thinkstock, b Levent Konuk / Shutterstock, c skynesher / iStockphoto, d Catlin Petolea / iStockphoto / Thinkstock, e Fuse / Thinkstock, f gchutka / iStockphoto, g CEFutcher / iStockphoto, h gbh007 / iStockphoto; p50 t iStockphoto / Thinkstock, bl Viktar Malyshchyts / Shutterstock, br DanCardiff / iStockphoto; p56 Antonio M. Rosario / The Image Bank / Getty Images; p57 t Bettmann / CORBIS, c Jo Ann Snover / Shutterstock, b Triff / Shutterstock; p78 t Andrey Pavlov / Shutterstock, b Morley Read / iStock /Thinkstock; p79 t Dragisa Savic / iStock / Thinkstock, bNachteule/ Thinkstock; p82 t-b Africa Studio / Shutterstock, sofiaworld / iStock / Thinkstock, Raul Souza / iStock / Thinkstock, zorani / iStockphoto; p93 t DarioEgidi / iStockphoto, cl Maks Narodenko / Shutterstock, cr Gordon Bell / Shutterstock, bl Venus Angel / Shutterstock, br iStock/Thinkstock; p95 fotohunter / Shutterstock; p101 Blend Images / Alamy; p105 l-r Maks Narodenko / Shutterstock, pictafolio / iStockphoto, sunstock/Thinkstock, Tund / fotolia, Aigars Reinholds / Shutterstock, Mariyana Misaleva / Shutterstock; p106 t OPIS Zagreb / Shutterstock, c, CHEN WS / Shutterstock, b salajean / Shutterstock; p107, Anastasios71 / Shutterstock; p112 Roland IJdema / Shutterstock; p113 stanley45 / iStockphoto; p114 Oxford Scientific / Getty Images; p115 a Roland IJdema / Shutterstock, b stanley45 / iStockphoto, c Oxford Scientific / Getty Images; p116 l-r Antrey / fotolia, fovito / fotolia, Rich Carey / Shutterstock, Eric Isselée / fotolia, Pakhnyushchyy / fotolia, Eric Isselee / Shutterstock; p117 Petr Malyshev / Shutterstock; p123 Evgeniapp / Shutterstock; p124 Evgeniapp / Shutterstock; p127 t l-r Mihai-Bogdan Lazar / fotolia, Alexander Mackenzie / iStockphoto, Alexy Bykov/iStock/Thinkstock, bl David Bagnall / Alamy, br vovez/fotolia.

Key: t = top, c = centre, b = bottom, l = left, r = right

Development of this publication has made use of the Cambridge English Corpus (CEC). The CEC is a multi-billion word computer database of contemporary spoken and written English. It includes British English, American English and other varieties of English. It also includes the Cambridge Learner Corpus, developed in collaboration with Cambridge English Language Assessment. Cambridge University Press has built up the CEC to provide evidence about language use that helps to produce better language teaching materials.

This product is informed by the English Vocabulary Profile, built as part of English Profile, a collaborative programme designed to enhance the learning, teaching and assessment of English worldwide. Its main funding partners are Cambridge University Press and Cambridge English Language Assessment and its aim is to create a 'profile' for English linked to the Common European Framework of Reference for Languages (CEFR). English Profile outcomes, such as the English Vocabulary Profile, will provide detailed information about the language that learners can be expected to demonstrate at each CEFR level, offering a clear benchmark for learners' proficiency. For more information, please visit www.englishprofile.org